S-CORPORATION BEGINNER'S GUIDE

HOW TO SUCCESSFULLY FORM, MANAGE & MAINTAIN AN S-CORPORATION EVEN IF YOU'RE AN ABSOLUTE BEGINNER (A COMPLETE UP-TO-DATE & EASY-TO-FOLLOW GUIDE)

WALTER GRANT

CONTENTS

INTRODUCTION

"Taxation is the price which civilized communities pay for the opportunity of remaining civilized" (Bushnell Hart, n.d.). So said Albert Bushnell Hart, and he was right. This is why taxes are a reality that all American adults have to live with, especially those who own, or are looking to start, their own businesses. If you're looking to start your own business, figuring out how to do your taxes might be at the forefront of your mind. However, it is likely that this isn't the only thing on your mind. After all, you have a myriad of other matters to decide on before you can start considering taxes, such as which type of corporation you're going to start in the first place.

There are many different types of corporations and businesses a person can start in the United States. Deciding on which one might be difficult, especially if you aren't well-versed in the legal and business lingo that the corporate world entails. After doing some research, you might have landed upon the rough idea that you'd like to start an S-Corporation or S-Corp. You might be hesitant to take action on this matter because you're not certain what an S-Corp really is and how it works. You might have heard about some of the benefits that an S-Corp offers, like certain tax benefits, protecting your assets, and increasing your and your business' credibility. Yet, you might be uncertain as to what those benefits really entail and what kind of difference they might make for you and your new business in the long run.

Not everyone has a business degree or experience in starting a business. So, not everyone can be expected to immediately grasp the ins and outs of an S-Corp, which means it's understandable that you might hesitate to start one. It's equally understandable if you're hesitant to start your own S-Corp because of financial constraints. Starting a business can be a costly endeavor, especially if you start on the wrong foot. Those who know this may hesitate to start their own S-Corp. They might have a hard time accurately weighing the risks they will be taking and the rewards they stand to gain. On top of that, they might not be fully aware of the legal considerations that go into opening up and running an S-Corp. As an extension of that, they might experience considerable stress and anxiety as they try to figure out how to ensure their new corporation's longevity and well-being.

A final reason why an individual may experience some reluctance when it comes to starting their own S-Corporation is that they might not be able to fully grasp the risks involved. Truthfully, a great deal of risk comes with starting your own S-Corp, and most sources prove reluctant to reveal the full scope and nature of these risks to new entrepreneurs. This takes away their ability to make proper informed decisions. Thus, trying to start your own S-Corporation becomes akin to trying to find your way in unfamiliar territory while it's pitch black. At least, it would be if it wasn't for the book that you are currently holding in your hands.

My intention in writing the *S-Corporation Beginner's Guide* is to provide readers who are considering starting their own business with the beacon that they need as they navigate the pitch-black waters of the business world. It's to ensure they know all that they need to know before launching their new business so that they can take their next steps confidently. It's to help them properly weigh the risks and rewards that come with S-Corporations and make the best financial and business-related decisions for themselves. It's to lift the veil of mystery surrounding the many legal considerations that come with S-Corporations and aid readers as they conduct thorough and accurate risk management for their businesses. Put another way, *the S-Corporation Beginner's Guide's* true purpose is to be a guide and mentor to the readers who have a brilliant business idea and just need some help determining how to realize it.

Having written a similar book, the *LLC's Beginners' Guide*, and witnessed firsthand the tremendous amount of success it achieved, as well as how many people it was able to help, writing another book was a necessity and a calling for me. Considering my background in the business world, a new book designed to help entrepreneurs wanting to launch their own S-Corp seemed the most logical next step to me. The entrepreneurial journey that I have been through, successful though it might have been, I believe, predisposes me to write such a book and help readers who are at the start of their own unique journeys. After experiencing the many ups and downs of business ownership in the entrepreneurial world, it seems evident to me that by sharing my depth and breadth of knowledge, I can be of considerable help to readers.

As a child, I was considered a creative type, as opposed to someone who was business-oriented. Most people would say that I was off in my "own world" thanks to my vivid imagination. Often, I'd build random things and design the most unique creations with whatever materials I had around me. That creativity never left me. So, as I grew up, I moved from wanting to build things to wanting to build my own business one day. While I would go on to realize this ambition one day, the road I'd take to do so would neither prove to be easy nor quick. Instead, it would be one rife with hurdles and challenges. I took my first step toward walking that road five years after my graduation when I quit my corporate job. I went out on my own shortly thereafter and sought to start my first business.

Unfortunately, that business never took off, despite the fact that I poured two years of my life into it. In fact, things got bad enough that I had to file for bankruptcy. Despite this major setback, however, I refused to quit. Rather, I took this as an invaluable opportunity to learn and grow. After taking a short break to catch my breath and reflect on what went wrong, I got back on my feet, rolled up my sleeves, and started from zero once again. As I did, I put the things that I learned from my past mistakes to good use. Thus, I was able to keep from repeating them. Not only that, but I was able to quickly build a massively successful business, which I would later sell for a wonderful eight-figure sum.

It is on account of these experiences that I decided to write this book, as well as the one I wrote previously about starting an LLC. My goal in my writing is to create works that can help readers avoid the initial mistakes I made when I was first starting out as an entrepreneur. It's to arm them with the invaluable knowledge they need to ensure their businesses become true success stories. It's to clear away any confusion readers may have about what an S-Corp is, why they should start one, how they can do so, how to manage their company, and more.

S-Corp Beginners Guide, then, is meant to be a companion for budding entrepreneurs whose minds are brimming with ideas that they wish to translate into reality. It's meant to be a guide that will enable readers to avoid any outdated information out there that might mislead them in the ever-changing business world. Similarly, it's meant to be a beacon that can spare them a great deal of confusion by simplifying seemingly overcomplicated or overly vague information. Hence, this book is the perfect tool for you as you introduce yourself to the business world and take those first steps to form your own S-Corp so that it can become the mesmerizing success story it has the potential to become.

CHAPTER 1
WHAT IN THE WORLD IS AN S-CORPORATION?

We live in a world that seems to be dominated by businesses and corporations, at least in terms of sheer numbers. Look around in a city, any city, and you'll find that you are surrounded by a staggering number of businesses. Quickly delve into what type of businesses they are, and you'll make a surprising discovery: There is a shocking number of S-Corporations out there. To put things into context, presently, there are 7.4 million S-Corporations and C-Corporations, as well as 23 million sole proprietorships in the United States alone (Hodge, 2014). The number of S-Corps, C-Corps, and sole proprietorships has practically tripled since the 1980s.

So, why is this the case? Why have more and more people been starting up these kinds of businesses? If we want to understand this question, we must first grasp what, precisely, an S-Corp is, what it does, and what kinds of advantages it can offer its owner. In simple terms, an S-Corp is a business that is allowed to pass its taxable income, deductions, losses, and credits straight to the shareholders of the company (Kagan, 2019). That means that S-Corporations don't pay taxes. Rather, they make payments to their shareholders, who in turn pay their own taxes once tax season rolls around. For this to be the case, however, the corporation in question must have at most 100 shareholders. If a business has, say, 101 shareholders, it will not be able to do this, and thus, it will never qualify as an S-Corp.

Given this situation, S-Corps are considered to be pass-through entities, much like limited liability companies (LLCs) are. This is the very reason they're considered to be desirable among entrepreneurs, particularly those launching their first-ever companies. S-Corps are called S-Corps because of the Internal Revenue Service (IRS), an organization that's loved by all. The IRS has a specific subchapter, known as Subchapter S, that explains this shareholder tax situation, thus, the name.

Of course, having a certain number of shareholders isn't the only defining characteristic of S-Corps. There are others. One is that a company must have a board of directors in order to classify as an S-Corp. Another is that they must write their own company bylaws. Another is that they have to conduct regular shareholder meetings and keep minutes, that is to say, detailed notes, of every meeting, as well as of any company meeting that takes place.

Setting up an S-Corp is desirable to entrepreneurs for a variety of reasons, as we will see in detail in the following chapter. To briefly touch upon these benefits: it is obvious that S-Corps don't have to pay federal tax. S-Corps can be used to lower your personal income tax. This corporation model also allows for the transfer of interests or the adjustment of property without facing negative, tax-related consequences. Meanwhile, S-Corps allows shareholders to be considered "employees." This is good news because the shareholders can receive their corporate dividends, which are subject to much lower tax rates.

A final advantage that S-Corporations have to offer you is that they help establish credibility. They do so by demonstrating that the owner of the business has made a formal commitment to the business by making it into an S-Corp. This situation doesn't just raise business' credibility among shareholders, it does so among potential customers, employees, and even suppliers as well.

As a rule, an S-Corporation has to meet two specific requirements to earn its classification. The first of these requirements has to do with its size. An S-Corporation has, at max, 100 shareholders, as you have seen. That means that such a corporation is and must be a small business. In keeping with that, an S-Corp's structure cannot be overly complex. Hence, if an S-Corp wanted to expand the size of its operations, it would need to change its status to another type of corporation, such as a C-Corp, an entity you'll find out more about momentarily (Palmer, 2023).

The second requirement that an S-Corp needs to meet has to do with its location. To qualify as an S-Corp, a business must be founded in the United States. Such an entity can do some business with various international companies around the world. However, its shareholders must be US citizens, without exception.

A BRIEF HISTORY OF S-CORPS

S-Corporations may be a dominant kind of business in the United States these days, but they didn't use to be. In fact, S-Corps have existed for less than 100 years as they were first conceived in 1946. Before that, there were only two types of businesses entrepreneurs could start. The first of these was a partnership. The second was a sole proprietorship. Individuals who started partnerships faced two tiers of federal taxes: one on the corporate level and one on the individual one. Hence, they were rather unappealing, at least to most people. Individuals who started sole proprietorship weren't subject to this same treatment. Instead, they faced only a single layer of taxation. Unlike partnerships, though, sole proprietorships denied them liability protection. This made sole proprietorships rather unappealing for entrepreneurs, too.

Fortunately for many, the US Department of Treasury was well aware of these issues. So, in 1946, they suggested merging liability protection with a single-tier federal tax system in order to make it easier for people to start their own businesses. A couple of years after this suggestion was made, President Dwight Eisenhower took office. President Eisenhower was a Republican, but the House at the time was Democratic for the most part. Hence, it wasn't too surprising when the House started accusing President Eisenhower of engaging in trickle-down economics. For those of you who are not well-versed in economic terminology, that means the House accused the president of adopting and favoring policies that benefitted the already wealthy and large corporations exclusively.

The merits of the accusations aside, it was evident to both Democrats and Republicans at the time that large corporations seemed to have too much wealth and power in their hands and that the economic sphere was being dominated by a few choice businesses. In this economic environment, they observed that there were very few private businesses to speak of, an observation that served as an ill omen for the future of development and innovation. That observation, coupled with the House's opinions of President Eisenhower's policies, pushed the president to embrace the proposal that the US Treasury had made a few years earlier. So it was that the House, led by Democratic Finance Chairman Harry

Byrd at the time, created subchapter S of the tax code on President Eisenhower's recommendation. As the House created this subchapter, they decided to impose a few key limitations on this new type of business entity. These limitations were that such businesses had to:

- be founded and based in the United States.
- have no more than 100 shareholders.
- have shareholders that were exclusively based in the US.
- have only one class of stock that they could offer to shareholders.

Before the House created subchapter S, thereby giving birth to S-Corporations, the top income tax rate for individuals was 91% (Staes, n.d.). Meanwhile, that same rate was around 51% for corporations. Consequently, the federal tax rate of a shareholder who had a median household income equaled 60% of their income, if not more, thanks to double taxation. The elimination of this devastating situation would mark a new beginning for entrepreneurship and small business ownership in the country. Over the years, S-Corporations would become immensely popular in all states. According to the IRS' current estimates, there are more than five million S-Corporations within the nation, and that figure will likely continue to rise as the years go by.

Naturally, there is some competition between S-Corps and LLCs in that individuals wanting to start their own businesses often get caught between the two. Given the unique tax benefits that come with LLCs, which are explored in my other book regarding LLCs, this confusion is understandable. So is the fact that there are about 2.5 million LLCs in the United States currently, whereas there only used to be about 120,000 of them in 1995 (Staes, n.d).

As with any business entity, S-Corps have evolved and changed significantly over the years, though their key defining characteristics and requirements have remained the same. For instance, about four decades after S-Corps first came onto the scene, their definition was expanding, allowing certain banks to be considered S-Corps too (De & Mehran, 2014). When Congress first conceived S-Corps, they declared that commercial banks could not be placed into this category of business. Their argument for this was that banks already enjoyed certain tax benefits and, therefore, didn't need to be classified as an S-Corporation. However, banks started challenging this assertion in 1993. Thanks to their lobbying efforts, a new law called the Small Business Job Protection Act was passed in 1996. This act decreed that any bank whose assets equaled less than $500 million and that had a reserve method for accounting for bad debts could organize themselves into a S-Corporation, so long as they abided by the typical requirements of S-Corps, such as the the number of shareholders they could have.

To be clear, this isn't the only change that S-Corporations have undergone, nor will it be the only change they will ever experience. In fact, S-Corporations are likely in for a few more evolutions, especially when you consider that they are at the very heart of certain economic debates that are ongoing today. A lot of these economic debates center on tax reform and reducing the tax rates that are applied to businesses (Staes, n.d.). They are similarly part of discussions regarding why there haven't been any significant increases in wages in recent years despite the fact that wealthy businesses only seem to be getting wealthier. S-Corporations remain at the core of both of these debates because of their unique structure.

It is this structure that has allowed S-Corps to migrate from corporate tax codes to individual ones, a state of affairs that significantly distorts distribution tables. Of course, the fact that the House has continually been relaxing the rules by which S-Corporations are governed for the past 50 years or so plays a part in this as well. The rules that apply to S-Corporations have changed, implying that S-Corporations have changed, too. They likely will continue changing as the world that we live in and the rules it's governed by keep evolving. Consequently, S-Corporations' popularity among the different business entities out there may change and evolve as well.

S-CORPS VS. OTHER BUSINESSES

How do S-Corporations currently stack up against other business types? There are many different kinds of businesses you can open up, as you know. Of these, S-Corps can most easily be compared to LLCs, which are their biggest competitor in a way, as well as C-Corporations and sole proprietorships. To start with the first, an LLC is a pass-through tax entity, much like S-Corps. As such, it's a type of business entity that small business owners, particularly those who are newcomers to the business world, often opt for.

Generally speaking, LLCs and S-Corps have a number of similarities. For instance, they both afford their owners limited liability protection. That means that the owners of S-Corps and LLCs typically aren't considered to be personally responsible for any debts or other liabilities their businesses incur. S-Corps and LLCs are also pass-through entities, as mentioned before. A pass-through entity is one where businesses don't have to pay income tax. Instead, whatever profit or loss a business makes is passed on to the owners' and shareholders' personal tax returns. This helps owners and shareholders avoid the double taxation that can otherwise put them in a chokehold.

A final similarity between LLCs and S-Corps is that they are both subject to certain requirements in order for owners and shareholders to enjoy the privileges they can afford. For S-Corporations, that means being based and founded in the US, having your shareholders be from and in the US, and not having more than 100 shareholders. For LLCs, that means having a registered agent, filing annual reports, and paying certain annual fees. Some of these LLC requirements are applicable to S-Corporations, too, as you'll see in the coming chapters.

While LLCs and S-Corporations are similar in a number of ways, there are a couple of key factors that set them apart from one another. One of these factors is that LLCs can have an unlimited number of members, including shareholders. In other words, they don't have to cap their shareholders at 100. Another key difference is that non-US citizens can be members of LLCs. Non-US citizens cannot, however, be members of S-Corps, a fact that we've made note of already. Meanwhile, LLCs are permitted to have various subsidiaries without any restrictions being applied to them. The same cannot be said for S-Corps (Nelson, 2023).

One very interesting difference between S-Corps and LLCs has to do with ownership of the entity. As a rule, LLCs can only be owned by people, that is to say living, breathing human beings. S-Corps, however, can be owned by other corporations, other LLCs, trusts, or partnerships.

LLCs are allowed to have more than one kind of stock. That means they can offer different varieties of stock with different financial rights to shareholders. S-Corporations are unable to do this. Hence, they're unable to provide shareholders with a distribution preference, while LLCs can. As an extension of that, S-Corps' stocks are freely transferable. LLCs' stocks, however, are not, that is, as long as an LLC's operation agreement doesn't outline some guidelines for stock transfer.

One of the most catching differences between S-Corps and LLCs has to do with taxes, which makes sense, given how vital a part of the business world taxes are. Both S-Corporations and LLCs allow for self-employment taxes. However, the self-employment tax rates for S-Corps are slightly better than those for LLCs. This is because the owner of an S-Corp is treated as a paid employee, whereas this isn't necessarily the case for the owner of an LLC. Hence, S-Corp owners are able to avoid FICA taxes and treat their corporate earnings as unearned income subject to self-employment taxes.

The final difference between LLCs and S-Corps has to do with the way in which profits and losses are allocated. The shareholders and owners of S-Corporations typically receive their profit or loss as it corresponds to their percentage of ownership of the business. The profit that someone who owns 50% of an S-Corp's stock is, therefore, different than the profit that someone who owns 10%. LLCs' profits and losses, on the other hand, aren't distributed exclusively according to owners' and shareholders' percentage of ownership. Instead, an LLC may designate its own unique profit-loss distribution system as long as everyone agrees to it beforehand.

How about S-Corporations and C-Corporations, then? These two entities have a number of similarities between them as well. Before we delve into them, though, let's first understand what a C-Corp is. A C-Corp is the default corporation type according to IRS rules. They're essentially business entities that have obtained a special tax status, which affords them certain privileges and benefits that make them a desirable option to consider.

As with LLCs, S-Corps and C-Corps are similar in a number of ways. For starters, they both afford their owners limited liability protection so that said owners never become personally responsible for any liabilities their businesses incur. Similarly, both entities are businesses that can be created by state filing. The files to create an S-Corp or C-Corp are known as Articles of Incorporation. Also known as Certificates of Incorporation, these forms remain unchanged, regardless of whether you're founding an S-Corp or a C-Corp.

Another similarity between C-Corps and S-Corps can be observed between their structures. These business entities have owners, shareholders, directors, and officers. The shareholders in question own the corporation. However, the business' actual owner is the corporation itself, which is why these two businesses are able to afford shareholders limited liability protection. Shareholders typically elect a board of directors for the business and task them with overseeing operations, directing all major business affairs, and making the important decisions that need to be made. This board, however, isn't usually responsible for day-to-day operations.

A final similarity between C-Corps and S-Corps has to do with their compliance responsibilities. Both S-Corps and C-Corps have to fulfill certain internal and external obligations, such as issuing stock and adopting certain bylaws. Otherwise, they cannot legally fulfill their business.

S-Corps and C-Corps may be similar in a variety of ways, but there are some important distinctions between them. To begin with, the most obvious is that S-Corps and C-Corps are taxed very differently. S-Corps get to avoid federal taxation, as you know. C-Corps do not. Instead, they file Tax Return Form 1120 and pay taxes at the corporate level (Huston, 2022). If they distribute corporate income to owners as dividends, they potentially face double taxation. S-Corps allowing owners to skip this potentiality altogether is one of the many reasons why they're considered desirable among small business owners.

Unlike S-Corporations, C-Corps don't have a cap on how many shareholders they can have. They, likewise, aren't subject to any requirements where their shareholders are concerned. Hence, an individual doesn't have to be a US citizen to be able to become a shareholder in a C-Corp. Finally, like LLCs, C-Corps are able to offer multiple classes of stock to people. S-Corps are only able to offer one type.

As you can gather from all that, S-Corps hold certain advantages over C-Corps. One is that they only have a single layer of taxation to them. Another is that pretty significant tax cuts, as much as 20% to be specific, are typically offered to S-Corps. Still, another is that S-Corps can pass through their losses to their shareholders, thereby offsetting their income, if need be. These all make S-Corps a very appealing option to consider. However, this doesn't mean that C-Corps don't have their own particular drawcards. That they can have an unlimited number of shareholders is one of them. There's also the fact that C-Corps have a lower maximum tax rate, which can make things significantly easier and more pleasant for owners and shareholders. Add to that that C-Corps can have an easier time than S-Corps to obtain financing, and it's easy to see the general appeal of the business entity. Still, given the danger of double taxation for C-Corps, most small business owners and new business owners opt for S-Corps over C-Corps or sole proprietorships.

A final business entity type you may consider is a sole proprietorship. A sole proprietorship is a business entity where a singular, that is to say sole, individual owns the company in question. As such, they pay personal income taxes for their business. In doing so, they are held liable for any damages or liability that their business incurs. That, understandably, is a drawback inherent to sole proprietorships but not found in S-Corps, seeing as it can put a person's personal assets in danger (Rogers, n.d.). There is an upside to this matter, though: It's that sole proprietorships are single entities, not separate ones. That's important because it can spare owners from having to pay and deal with the licensing fees and other similar operating fees they'd have to pay to launch their S-Corp.

Another appeal to sole proprietorships has to do with their overall structure. Sole proprietorships don't need to be structured in the way traditional businesses are to be able to operate properly. Hence, they don't need components like bookkeepers, business bank accounts, or even employees. The sole proprietor operating the sole proprietorship will usually be more than enough.

A final benefit of sole proprietorships is that any income they make flows directly to the sole proprietor. That is after taxes, of course, and those taxes can be quite high, especially if owners have to deal with double taxation. With this possibility in the air, many sole proprietors tend to hire tax advisors just to make sure they can navigate these complicated waters correctly. Obviously, this isn't something that S-Corp owners and shareholders have to deal with. They likewise don't have to deal with the same liability risks that come with sole proprietorships.

COMMON MISCONCEPTIONS ABOUT S-CORPS

As you can see, there are many reasons why an individual might prefer an S-Corp over other business entities. There are some reasons that can cause them to hesitate to do so, as well. However, it must be noted here that some of these reasons aren't wholly accurate. Instead, there are misconceptions surrounding S-Corps that cloud people's judgment of them. One of these misconceptions, for instance, is that S-Corps are formed in the same way that regular corporations are formed. This is not the case. Forming an S-Corp is significantly easier and simpler than forming most types of corporations, as you'll see in the coming chapters. Hence, if this is a source of hesitation for you, it really shouldn't be (Murray, 2019).

Not all misconceptions about S-Corps give rise to such hesitation, of course. Some just cause potential S-Corp owners to misunderstand how their corporation is supposed to work, which can be a critical mistake to make. One such misconception is that S-Corporations work the exact same way LLCs do when it comes to taxes. This is not the case. The way that S-Corps and LLCs pay their taxes is similar in that they minimize the liability that the business in question is placed under. However, there are nuances that make the process different for S-Corporations. Each owner or shareholder in an S-Corp has to file a form called Schedule K-1 to file their taxes. This form shows their personal share of net income. Said income is usually added to the owner or shareholder's personal tax return.

Speaking of taxes, a final important misconception about S-Corporations is that their owners don't have to pay self-employment taxes. This is patently untrue, seeing as S-Corporation owners who work in their businesses have to pay FICA taxes. S-Corporation owners additionally have to pay themselves a reasonable and fair salary, which is, again, taxable.

SUMMARY BOX

Now that you know the basics about what an S-Corp is and what it isn't, you're ready to delve into the specifics and start exploring what makes S-Corps perfect for you. Before we do that, however, let's quickly summarize what we have learned:

- An S-Corp is a business that is allowed to pass its taxable income, deductions, losses, and credits straight to the shareholders of the company.
- S-Corps can only have 100 shareholders at maximum, and all of these shareholders must be US citizens based in the United States.
- S-Corps don't have to pay federal taxes and are typically able to avoid double taxation.
- S-Corps are very appealing to small business owners and new business owners because they are pass-through entities, much like LLCs. This fact accounts for their very popularity.

CHAPTER 2
HOW TO KNOW IF AN S-CORPORATION IS THE PERFECT FIT FOR YOU

"Only those who will risk going too far can possibly find out how far one can go."

T. S. ELIOT

So, you've found a fantastic business idea, and you're certain that it can succeed. You just need to actually launch your company to make sure that happens. You've started doing some research on S-Corporations to better understand how they work and see if this business structure might be the right fit for you. In truth, you're considering a couple of options for your business, but the more you think about it, the more starting an S-Corp seems to be the right path for you. Is that really the case, though? This is a question you have to consider very carefully, as this choice may very well play a determinant role in your success or your failure, for that matter, as I discovered through bitter experience.

Don't get me wrong: S-Corporations are very sound business models to go for, especially for small business owners and those who are new to the business scene. However, deciding to start an S-Corp without fully grasping its advantages and disadvantages can be catastrophic. At best, this situation can slow down your progress considerably and force you to contend with a very steep learning curve. At worst, it can cause you to get caught unawares by disadvantages you hadn't been aware of in the past, thereby leading to your business' ultimate failure. Fortunately, avoiding all this is well within your hands, so long as you're willing to do the necessary research. Seeing as you've picked this book up and made it to this chapter already, you clearly are ready and willing to do so. That being the case, here are all the most vital advantages S-Corporations stand to offer you, as well as all the drawbacks they might have, clearly laid out for you like ducks in a row.

ADVANTAGES OF S-CORPORATIONS

By now, you're familiar with some of the advantages that S-Corporations can offer you. One of those advantages is that S-Corporations offer limited liability to owners and shareholders. That means that they prevent owners and shareholders from incurring any personal damages should things go wrong. For instance, suppose that you're an owner or shareholder of an S-Corp and said S-Corp has incurred a number of debts. Since the company is an S-Corp, your personal assets won't be touched by those who come to collect on that debt, at least for the most part, as there are exceptions. One exception is for companies whose business is giving advice to others. Should such a business give incorrect advice to its clients, causing them to incur damages, then shareholders' and owners' personal assets may become at risk, given the fact that the company will be at fault (*The Advantages & Disadvantages of S Corporations*, 2021).

As mentioned previously, S-Corporations are pass-through entities. Hence, they are able to pass their income, profit, and losses onto their shareholders and owners. Thus, they can avoid major damages to the company and avoid federal taxation. Once they pass their income to shareholders and owners, those individuals then pay their share of the company's profits on their personal income tax returns, which are subject to a personal income tax rate (Huston, 2022a).

Another obvious advantage of S-Corporations is that they afford you a certain degree of flexibility when it comes to profit distribution. As you'll recall, the profits and losses of an S-Corp can be freely distributed to its owners, according to the percentage of shares they hold. For instance, if a shareholder owns 30% of the shares and another holds 40%, then profits and losses will be divided 30/40 between them. That kind of flexibility can be very advantageous. It can, for example, spare your business from incurring staggering damages should it experience some losses, keeping them from impacting the performance too much. Similarly, it can allow shareholders and owners to claim a great deal of profit, which isn't exactly something that they would have cause to complain about (Kagan, 2019).

The way in which profits and losses are distributed to shareholders and owners can benefit them come tax season as well. As you'll recall, the shareholders of an S-Corp can be considered the employees of a business. They can, therefore, draw salaries the way employees can. Likewise, they can receive dividends from their S-Corp, along with other kinds of distributions. These can help them to reduce the self-employment tax liability they're under. At the same time, they can reduce wages-paid deductions for the corporation while allowing it to continue to generate a profit.

S-Corporations give a certain degree of credibility to shareholders, as you know. This credibility is very important for attracting customers to the business and also attracting good, hardworking employees. It's also vital for attracting investors to the business, which can help it to grow and develop significantly. The way in which S-Corporations are structured can be another favorable factor for potential investors, helping to attract more investors and thus have an easier time both getting the company off the ground and expanding it should you choose to do so.

There are a couple of additional benefits that S-Corporations can offer owners and shareholders, like the fact that it keeps their personal and business assets separate. Personal assets can include anything from a shareholder's personal bank account to their personal property. Being a shareholder in an S-Corp usually means that such personal assets cannot be seized because of business liabilities. This is a source of assurance for many investors, shareholders, and owners. After all, no one wants to put everything they have at risk by becoming a shareholder of a company.

In some ways, S-Corporations are very easy to manage. In keeping with that, they're easy to terminate if and when you decide to do so. This is the final benefit that this type of company has to offer. Voluntarily terminating an S-Corp requires getting at least 50% of the company's shareholders to vote to do so. If you are able to do that, then you'll be able to terminate your S-Corp easily and at your discretion.

DRAWBACKS OF S-CORPORATIONS

Having said all that, S-Corps do have some unique drawbacks or disadvantages, just as any business category does. You must take these drawbacks into consideration before you decide to start an S-Corp. Otherwise, you could risk being caught unaware by a drawback and suffer the consequences, which can be grave. The first drawback that S-Corps has is that they are subject to much stricter eligibility requirements than other businesses. These restrictions are largely applicable to an S-Corp's transfer of ownership. The owner of an S-Corp may try to transfer their ownership to someone else in order to maintain their status as a pass-through entity. However, they might find that they are unable to do so because of the restrictions they're placed under. This is an important matter to be aware of, especially if a transfer of ownership is something you would consider down the line.

Another type of restriction that S-Corps are placed under has to do with their stock. S-Corporations can only offer one type of stock, as you know, though those stocks can be both voting and non-voting, respectively. What this means is that investors cannot be offered different distribution rights or dividends. This is coupled with another restriction that's placed on shareholders, which is that an S-Corp cannot have more than 100 shareholders. An S-Corp looking to expand beyond that will, therefore, have to consider switching to a different business structure.

Shareholders can be given their dividends in different proportions, as mentioned previously. This is largely an advantage, but it's one that comes with a greater disadvantage in the form of higher scrutiny on the part of the IRS. In S-Corps, the IRS closely watches the payments that are made to shareholders. In doing so, they will strive to make sure that they are always characterized in one way or another when payments are characterized or recharacterized as dividends, which can cost the company a deduction for the compensation that is being paid to shareholders. When payments are characterized or recharacterized as wages, then this will make the company subject to employment tax liabilities.

There's a negative consequence that comes with only being permitted to have one class of stock, the way S-Corps are. This consequence is that it makes S-Corporations less flexible when it comes to how they can allocate losses and profits to shareholders. Shareholders' profits and losses are determined by the percentage of shares they hold. Hence, a shareholder cannot earn more than their percentage allows. This can put them at a disadvantage, especially since such a restriction isn't imposed on other types of businesses, such as LLCs. After all, LLCs can be taxed as partnerships, meaning that the profits or losses that are allocated to their shareholders can be determined in an operating agreement that will be written as the LLC is being founded.

The restrictions that are imposed on S-Corporations aren't the sole culprits behind the disadvantages that come with them. There are other culprits at hand, such as expenses. Forming and managing an S-Corp can be a costly endeavor. The process, as you'll see in later chapters, will start with you filing your Articles of Incorporation to incorporate your business. You'll have to pay some fees for that. This step will be followed by finding a registered agent and paying the necessary fees for that as well. Additional state-related fees, which will change depending on where exactly you're located, will follow soon thereafter. Now, granted, you will be able to deduct the cost of these expenses in tax season, but operating your business will still take some level of monetary investment. That's a fact you have to bear in mind as you launch your business and plan for the days ahead.

One disadvantage to consider is your S-Corporation's assessment. More specifically, it has to do with its appreciated assets. Appreciated assets are assets whose values increase over time, such as your corporation's stocks. The thing about such assets is that you have to generate a tax bill for them. You have to do this in order to distribute those assets' earnings to yourself and your corporation's co-owners and shareholders. Without such a bill, moving forward with the distribution process will not be possible, no matter how much value your appreciated assets earn.

Speaking of assets, trying to withdraw any from an S-Corporation can be a bit of a nightmare, at least administratively speaking. The same goes for withdrawing money from an S-Corporation. When withdrawing money or assets, you have to characterize that withdrawal as a dividend, loan, compensation, or another type of payment. You have to do so for tax purposes, as you might have guessed. If you're characterizing the withdrawal as compensation, then you'll have payroll taxes that will be due in tax season. So, you'll need to file the required W-2 forms and file your payroll tax returns. Meanwhile, if you're characterizing the withdrawal as a loan, then you'll need to prepare the necessary loan document (*The Advantages & Disadvantages of S Corporations*, 2021). Based on that, you can see why a withdrawal of this nature can be frustrating, to say the least.

A final disadvantage to S-Corps is that most of the benefits that the company provides to owners and shareholders are taxable, at least so long as said owners or shareholders own more than two percent of the company they're involved in. This can prove to be irritating at best and draining, monetarily speaking, at worst, which is why it must be carefully managed (Huston, 2022a).

WHO NEEDS AN S-CORPORATION

Clearly, there are many disadvantages to S-Corporations. Yet, these disadvantages do not eliminate the obvious benefits and advantages that accompany this type of business model. To be clear, every business type and model out there has benefits and disadvantages that are wholly unique to them. Attempting to find one that won't have any downsides will not work. The trick is to find disadvantages you can live and work with. It's to figure out how to manage those drawbacks and get the most out of the benefits the model you're opting for has to offer you. This begs some important questions, like, who should start an S-Corp rather than some other type of business? Whose needs do S-Corps serve the most? Who will benefit the most from them, and how will they not be as impacted by their disadvantages as others might be?

As a rule, S-Corps are a great business model for small business owners. However, that doesn't mean that it's a good option for every small business owner. If you want to figure out whether an S-Corp is the right model for you, you have to ask certain questions of yourself, starting with, "Am I able to cover the additional costs that will come with starting such a company?" After all, S-Corps can be an expensive business to start, as previously established. If you're starting an S-Corp, then at a minimum, you're going to have to pay (Smiles, 2019):

- A salary to yourself as the owner, so long as your business is actually making money, the amount of which will be up to your discretion. If the business isn't making money yet, then owners won't have to pay themselves salaries until it is.

- Payroll processing fees, which can be around $45 per month.
- Payroll taxes, meaning FICA, which typically amount to 7.35% of annual salary, as well as FUTA taxes, which amount to around 6% of the first $75,000 you earn.

Aside from these, you may incur some additional expenses, like:

- Annual state fees, which can amount to anything from $10 to $800, depending on which state you're in.
- Tax preparation fees once tax season arrives.
- Insurance costs as certain states require that you get insurance for your S-Corp.
- Accounting and bookkeeping costs, which will change depending on what your accountant or bookkeeper, two individuals or businesses you should hire given the scrutiny S-Corps are typically under, charges you.

So, knowing all the different costs that can accompany S-Corps, the key question you have to ask yourself is whether, realistically speaking, you can afford them. If the answer to that question is "yes," then an S-Corp might be the right type of business structure for you. If it's "no" or if you remain skeptical, then looking into other, more affordable business structures may be a good idea.

Like the first, the second question you have to ask yourself is related to your finances, too. This question is, "How much taxable income do I currently have?" One of the most appealing features of S-Corporations is that they have great tax-saving potential, as you well know. However, that potential won't be so appealing anymore if it turns out that your S-Corp's overall cost—as in the cost of paying payroll taxes, running payroll, and forming the actual S-Corp itself—surpasses your tax savings. The same can be said if your company's net profit remains minimal once the owner's salary has been deducted from it.

Your S-Corp needs to be capable of making a certain amount of money to avoid these two situations. While there are many opinions about this matter, the general consensus is that an S-Corp should make at least $75,000 in profits, that is to say, taxable income annually (Smiles, 2019). That way, they can avoid these situations and, thus, keep themselves out of hot water. So, if you're thinking of starting an S-Corp, then the logical thing to do is ask whether you can realistically earn such a sum annually. Based on the answer you give, you can decide whether you want to opt for this business structure or keep looking for an alternative.

A third question you may have concerns your business goals. Mainly, they have to do with what those goals are. Take your future ambitions, for example. How large do you want your S-Corp to eventually become? Where do you want to see your business in five- or ten years' time? Now, as you consider these, factor in the unique restrictions that are applied to S-Corps. This business structure can only have 100 shareholders at max. Those shareholders must be US citizens based in the US. An S-Corp cannot be owned by a partnership or corporation. Those restrictions have some interesting implications for your business's growth potential and ability. They hold similar implications for finding investors for your business, as well as any scenario where a company wants to buy yours. Given those facts, you have to consider what you want for your business's future very carefully. You have to consider whether those wants align with the restrictions placed upon S-Corps. If they do, then there's no issue with you starting your own S-Corp. If they don't, then perhaps you need to either find another business structure that works for you or revisit your goals for the future.

The final question you have to ask yourself has to do with your cash flow. Essentially, you have to ask yourself how consistent your cash flow actually is, especially since S-Corps pay both payroll taxes and the owner's salary. A great many S-Corps start struggling to survive, let alone thrive, shortly after their founding because they don't give due consideration to their cash flow. As such, they don't take the measures they need to take to ensure that their cash flow is steady and stable. Pretty soon, they run into payment issues and begin struggling financially. If you want to avoid such a situation, which you do, then your cash flow situation is one that merits careful consideration, particularly before you launch your company.

SUMMARY BOX

Say that you have considered all your options carefully, and after weighing the pros and cons of starting your own S-Corp, you've decided to go ahead with it. How exactly do you start an S-Corporation, then? What are you supposed to do, and how are you supposed to proceed? These will be the focal points of the next chapter. Before we delve into them, though, let's quickly summarize what we have learned in this chapter:

- Like any business structure, S-Corps have unique benefits to offer and disadvantages that come with them. One of those advantages is that S-Corporations offer limited liability to owners and shareholders, preventing owners and shareholders from incurring any personal damages should things go wrong.

- S-Corporations are pass-through entities. Hence, they are able to pass their income, profit, and losses onto their shareholders and owners.
- S-Corporations give a certain degree of credibility to shareholders, as you know. This credibility is very important for attracting customers and good, hardworking employees to your business. It's also vital for attracting investors to the business.
- Being a shareholder in an S-Corp usually means that such personal assets cannot be seized because of business liabilities. This is a source of assurance for many investors, shareholders, and owners.
- The owner of an S-Corp may try to transfer their ownership to someone else to maintain their status as a pass-through entity. However, they might find that they are unable to do so because of the restrictions they're placed under.
- S-Corporations can only offer one type of stock, though those stocks can be both voting and non-voting, respectively. What this means is that investors cannot be offered different distribution rights or dividends.
- In S-Corps, the IRS will, usually, closely watch the payments that are being made to shareholders. In doing so, they will strive to make sure that they are always characterized in one way or another.
- If you want to figure out whether an S-Corp is the right model for you, you have to ask, "Am I able to cover the additional costs that will come with starting such a company?"
- In considering S-Corps as a business structure, you must make sure your company is capable of making at least $75,000 in profits.

- Before you form your S-Corp, you must consider your business goals carefully and decide whether the restrictions placed on S-Corps will allow you to meet those goals.
- Finally, you must question whether you have a steady cash flow in your business before launching your S-Corp, especially since S-Corps pay both payroll taxes and the owner's salary.

CHAPTER 3
FORMING AN S-CORPORATION—YOUR PLAYBOOK

If you've considered your business structure options carefully and decided that starting an S-Corp is the way to go for you, then congratulations! You've taken the first step you need to take to make your business idea a reality. You've also joined the ranks of many successful individuals whose entrepreneurial journeys started out in much the same way yours has. There are all sorts of individuals among these entrepreneurs. There's the average Joe, the owner of that mom-and-pop store you used to love, your neighbors two doors down. There are even celebrities who choose to become S Corps or LLCs themselves, as odd as that might sound. Obviously, that's not what you are going to do, but you will be starting your own S-Corporation. So, how do you get that process started? What do you do to fully incorporate your business? What requirements are you supposed to meet, and how are you supposed to navigate the process as a whole? Well, let's find out.

HOW TO FORM AN S-CORPORATION: A STEP-BY-STEP PROCESS

Starting your own business always seems like a rather daunting process. However, this isn't necessarily true, at least not where S-Corps are concerned. Starting an S-Corp is actually a pretty straightforward, and easy, process. All you need to do is follow ten basic steps, one after another. The general steps that you have to take to launch your very own S-Corporation are:

1. Choosing the perfect name for your business.
2. Filing your Articles of Incorporation.
3. Issuing your S-Corp stock.
4. Forming your board of directors and appointing your directors.
5. Making sure to meet all other S-Corp requirements.
6. Getting your Employer Identification Number (EIN).
7. Choosing your S-Corp status.
8. Getting your state and federal S-Corp licenses.
9. Creating your S-Corp bylaws.
10. Scheduling your annual meetings and making sure to hold them.

The process for starting your own S-Corp starts with you choosing a name, as you can see. "What's in a name?" you might be wondering, to quote Shakespeare a bit. The short answer to that question is "many things." After all, your name is your brand. It's how people will know you and what they will call you once you enter into the marketplace. Hence, it's important that you choose the perfect name for your business. That perfect name must be unique. That isn't just important for the sake of standing out among your competitors. It's important because you are not allowed to choose a name that some other company has already taken. In other words, you can't exactly go ahead and name your company "Microsoft," at least not if you don't want to get into trouble.

Hang on, though. How can you know for sure whether a name that you're considering has already been chosen by some company or not? You can do so by checking your local Secretary of State's website. Here, you'll find a registry of names. This registry will contain every company name that has already been registered with the state. If a name is on this registry, you may not use it. If it's not included there, you can go ahead and use it however you wish. That means you can go ahead and register your name for yourself. As you're registering your name on the Secretary of State's website, you will have to follow certain simple guidelines. These guidelines will vary from state to state. However, it won't be hard to follow the rules. One basic rule that is found in pretty much every state is that your chosen name cannot include any profanity in it. Another is that it cannot include any terms or words that would mislead the public (Shopify Staff, 2023).

What if you're not 100% sure about what you want your name to be? In this case, you can choose what's known as a "doing business as" (DBA) name. This will be your temporary name, which you have to register as well, that you can use to your heart's content until you land upon the true name you want to take on.

Having chosen and registered your name or your DBA, you'll be able to file your Articles of Incorporation. What does that mean? This is the official step you need to take to start your S-Corporation, and it entails going to the IRS website. There, you will declare where you intend to incorporate your new business. As for what the actual file you'll be filing will include, Articles of Incorporation typically provide the following information:

- Your business name.
- A short description of what your business will be doing and what its main purpose is.
- Who your registered agent is—more on that later—and what their physical address in the state is.
- A short description of what kind of structure your business will have, including how many shares it will be permitted to issue.

Articles of Incorporation are typically no longer than a single page. As you can see, as far as official documents go, they're pretty simple and easy to write, so long as you know what you want your business to be about. Most states actually offer template Articles of Incorporation for entrepreneurs to use, thereby making things even simpler. You can find such templates on the Secretary of State's website. Once the form is filled out, you'll file it with your Secretary of State, paying a filing fee as you do so.

This will bring you to the next step of the process, which is to start issuing stock for your new corporation. You can start issuing stock either in the form of actual physical, that is to say, paper, certificates, or in the form of electronic certificates. This being the internet age, odds are that you'll go with the latter.

Now, this part of the process will have to be navigated a little carefully because S-Corps stocks have to meet some very strict requirements, as you know. One requirement that we've mentioned a few times is that S-Corps can only issue one type of stock. This means that S-Corps aren't allowed to issue preferred stocks like dividend priority. Instead, they must offer common stock with voting rights. The second requirement that S-Corp stocks must meet is that the shareholders getting them must be US citizens or, at the very least, residents. Non-resident aliens, then, cannot get said stock. A final requirement to abide by here is that only individuals, that is to say, living, breathing human beings, can purchase S-Corp stocks. Other corporations aren't allowed to do so.

Assuming you meet all these requirements, you can draw your stock certificates. These certificates will clearly state what a singular share is worth and the number of shares that are available for purchase. It will also include the following information:

- The name of the shareholder getting the share.
- The number of shares being sold to them.
- The determined price per share.
- The overall value of the shares that are sold.
- Which assets are being used to purchase the shares, and what their value is.
- The name or signature of an officer or director within the company.
- The name and signature of a witness bearing testimony to the sale.
- The date when the transaction takes place.

If you're still unsure as to what a stock certificate is supposed to look like, you're in luck. There are a myriad of templates you can find online. The Northwest Registered Agent, for example, have some very useful templates you can turn to.

When your stock certificates are stocked—pun intended—and ready to go, you can move on to the next step, which is to make sure you meet all the other S-Corp eligibility requirements. These requirements are provided to you by your good friend, the IRS. Fortunately, they make things pretty simple, too. One requirement they have is that financial institutions such as insurance companies cannot be S-Corps. So, if you're planning to open a financial organization, then odds are, you won't be able to make it into an S-Corp. As you've seen, there are exceptions to this rule, like certain kinds of banks, but exceptions don't make the rule. So, checking whether your business is eligible to classify as an S-Corp is always a good idea. Another type of corporation that cannot be considered eligible is domestic, international sales corporations. The same goes for corporations founded outside the US or any businesses that have non-resident aliens as owners or shareholders.

If your business isn't affected by these limitations, then congratulations! Your business is eligible to be considered an S-Corp. That means you can officially get your employer identification number (EIN). Your EIN is a number you get from the IRS for tax purposes. Think of it as the business equivalent of your social security number (SSN). Getting your business EIN is of the utmost importance. This is because your EIN will allow you to do all manner of things, such as set up payroll to compensate the employees making up your S-Corp, build credit for your business, open a business bank account, and even apply for any local licenses and permits you may need.

Getting an EIN isn't a complicated matter at all. All you need to do is file IRS form SS-4, and you should have your number in no time. After that, you can focus on electing your S-Corp status. In other words, you can file Form 2553 with the IRS. This form, otherwise known as Election by a Small Business Corporation, must be signed by all the shareholders in your company before it is filed. That's why you create and issue your stock certificates before you file this form. It's also why you'll need to put together your boardroom and elect your officers beforehand. Your board group is the group of individuals that will be governing your company. Electing such a body of governance is a must for S-Corps, especially since they are required to have at least one director. Once a full board of directors is formed, they'll be able to manage your business and take care of the important decisions that have to be made to secure its future. More to the point, they'll be able to sign the Election by a Small Business Corporation, thereby allowing you to file it.

Getting your EIN means acquiring any state and local permits and licenses you may need to run your S-Corp. As a most basic example, suppose that you're founding an S-Corp in the state of California. California's S-Corp rules dictate that if you want to do this, you have to file some additional documents, these being (Haegele, 2023):

- An Initial State of Information, which is a document you can file using form SI-550 and which you have to file once a year.
- An Operating Agreement, which is a document outlining your S-Corp's general structure, rules, regulations, provisions, and the overall way it will operate.

A number of states may require that S-Corps file documents such as the ones that California wants them to file. Given that, checking what the specific procedure for S-Corps is in your state and what, if any, additional forms they want you to fill out is a reasonable policy to adopt. At best, you'll discover you don't need to file anything extra and have an easy time, continuing on your merry way. At worst, it'll save you some time when you actually get started with this process and begin filing all that you need to. While you're checking your state's additional requirements, you should make a point of seeing whether you have to pay any corporate income taxes because some states impose their own. How much that tax rate can be varies from state to state. Similarly, some states require that you get certain permits and licenses to keep your S-Corp status. So, you should check if your state demands you have such permits and licenses, too. Assuming they do, you'll likely have to spend a modest sum acquiring them. You'll then be able to focus on actually launching and running your S-Corp with your mind at ease.

As you know, your penultimate step is to create your S-Corp bylaws. Otherwise known as your corporate bylaws, these are essentially your business' operating rules. These rules may include anything from when, how, and how often your board will meet to what your officer's responsibilities and roles will consist of to how a wide variety of administrative duties will be handled. It must be noted here that some states require by law that you create S-Corp bylaws. Others do not but still suggest that you do so. This is a good suggestion to follow, as your corporate bylaws can be vital for your business operations. They can ensure there's greater clarity to your operating procedures and decision-making process. They can help make sure you have limited liability at all times by making sure additional measures are taken for it. For instance, if you truly want to have limited liability protection, you must separate your business and personal assets. Having your corporate bylaws necessitates that owners do this, which can help them strengthen the limited liability protection that S-Corps gives them, a fact that you will come to truly appreciate if you ever find yourself having to go to court for any reason.

One good news about corporate bylaws is that unlike, say, your Articles of Incorporation, they do not need to be filed. Hence, you won't have to pay any filing fee for them. As for how you actually create your bylaws, as before, there are a variety of templates you can use online for this. Once you've used a template you trust to craft your bylaws, you should show them to a trusted lawyer. This is because your bylaws are considered legally binding documents. Ensuring they're sound and balanced from a legal standpoint before your board agrees to adopt them can help you avoid a lot of headaches later on. Once a lawyer has looked them over and made any recommendations they may have to make, you can show them to your board. Your board members can then formally adopt them. You can and should similarly show your bylaws to any and all shareholders so that they are made aware of your S-Corp's governing rules.

The last thing you have to do to start and run your own S-Corp is to hold annual board meetings. By law, you're required to schedule and run these meetings. So is keeping detailed notes, known as minutes, of each and every one of those meetings. These minutes are typically a good idea, as they allow you to keep careful track of all the decisions that are made in these meetings. They enable you to then act on these decisions with confidence. For the record, the decisions made in such meetings can be anything like appointing new boardroom members to solving important issues that crop up within your business.

One rule to keep in mind, both when you're having these meetings and when you're forming your board, is that many states require that more than half, that is to say, a quorum, of an S-Corp's shareholders be present in the annual boardroom meetings. Without this quorum, a meeting cannot truly be considered the "annual" meeting that you are supposed to be holding. That said, you can obviously have more than a quorum in your yearly boardroom meetings. You can likewise write a corporate bylaw dictating that a specific percentage of shareholders attend said meetings every year. Writing such a bylaw would ensure that you never fall short of the quorum requirement and that all shareholders are properly kept in the loop as to what's going on in your company.

ON REGISTERED AGENTS

As you may have noticed, we sort-of glossed over one of the steps that you have to take to form your own S-Corp, this step being finding a registered agent. To be more accurate, we glossed over what, precisely, a registered agent is and why S-Corps need them. In truth, this subject matter merits a closer, more thorough look because registered agents can have a vital, near life-saving role to play for S-Corps. First things first, though: What is a registered agent?

A registered agent is an individual or business that acts as your S-Corp's formal point of contact in all legal matters. They are the ones who receive legal documents on your S-Corporation's behalf. They are also the ones who receive communications from the state your S-Corp is in. Having received these materials, it's their duty to pass them on to you and your S-Corp.

One thing you'll notice when you're filing the necessary documents to form your S-Corp is that you will have to provide your state secretary with your chosen registered agent's name and address. That address will have to be somewhere within the state where your S-Corp is located. Say that you live in one state but want to register your S-Corp in another one altogether (CT Corporation Staff, 2023). This is something you are allowed to do, so long as you find a registered agent in the state where you're going to be launching your S-Corp. Say that your S-Corp expanded over the years and opened up different branches in different states without violating the 100 shareholders at max rule, of course. In that case, you're going to have to have a registered agent or statutory agent, as they're sometimes known, in each state your S-Corp has a presence in.

Suppose that you have an S-Corp, and someone has sadly decided to sue it. Papers will need to be delivered to your S-Corp for this to be possible. Your registered agent will be the one receiving those papers. Naturally, they'll have to get you those papers so that you are aware of what's going on and can take action as necessary. Whoever is suing you, in this case, will be able to get in touch with your registered agent because the fact that they are your agent will be a matter of public record. The same will go for your Secretary of State in the event that they have to contact your S-Corporation for any reason. More specifically, it will be true for the filing office of your Secretary of State, which may send your registered agent such files as annual reports, delinquency notices, or other similar documentation. Afterward, your agent will pass all these to your S-Corp.

Finding your registered agent is something you do very early on in the process you follow to launch your S-Corp. Typically, it's something you want to do before you file your Articles of Incorporation. This is because states usually don't accept and approve Articles of Incorporation if the individual filing them doesn't have a registered agent yet. They ascertain that you have a registered agent already by asking you to include their name and address in the state in the Articles themselves. They likewise ask that you include this information in your corporation's annual or biannual reports every time you issue them.

This is especially true in light of the fact that the registered agent you start with might not be the registered agent you continue working with in the years to come. Your registered agent might change for any number of reasons, after all. You might, for example, find that you're dissatisfied with their work. You might also learn that they'll be moving out of the state soon, which would mean they'd no longer be qualified to act as your agent once they've left.

Whatever the reason, in the event that your registered agent does change, you usually have to file a registered agent change form with the Secretary of State. Some states will allow you to simply declare the change on your annual reports without having to file such a form. So, the moment you realize you may have to change your agent, it's best to check whether this is true for your state or not. That way, you'll be able to take action quickly and without wasting any time. You'll be able to avoid incurring any penalties, which might happen if you fail to notify the state of the change at hand. In some places, failing to notify the state about a change in registered agents can result in the state actively dissolving your corporation.

Failing to notify the state about a change in registered agents can have a number of additional consequences. Say that your corporation is being sued. If you don't have a registered agent or haven't notified your state about a change in agents, you might not receive the summons you've been sent on time. At best, this will cost you valuable time, which you could have used to work on your defense. At worst, it can result in the plaintiff getting a default judgment against you, particularly if you do not show up for court. Even if you aren't sued, not notifying your state about your agent change in a timely fashion can cause you to lose your good standing with your state.

Of course, all that begs the question, "How do I find a registered agent?" To find a registered agent, you must first understand who can qualify as one. A registered agent can be anyone, so long as they live in the state your S-Corporation is in. A registered agent may also be another business or corporation. The one exception to this rule is that your S-Corporation cannot be its own registered agent. This being the only limitation that's placed on agents, finding one typically proves to be fairly easy. What if you want a professional registered agent, though? In this case, the agent that you choose will be someone you're going to be paying to be your agent. Hence, they should have the reputation and reliability to rise to the task that is given to them.

Additionally, they must be familiar with your corporation and its rules of compliance. They must know how to expertly handle Standard Operating Procedure papers, have a reliable and quick system for getting said papers to your corporation, and be capable of following up with you to make sure you got them safely. You can ascertain that an agent you're considering meets those qualifications by doing a little research about them. You should also be able to find plenty of potential agents by looking up professional registered agents within the state and conducting further research on them as well.

FORMING YOUR BOARD OF DIRECTORS

Another key step of the S-Corp process that merits a closer look is forming your board of directors. How do you go about forming such a board? How do you find qualified members for it and get them on board? What rules do you have to follow to structure and manage this board? These are all important questions to consider, seeing as your board is a group of individuals who will essentially be running your corporation. In an S-Corp, individual directors aren't able to sign contracts themselves and thus make decisions singlehandedly. Instead, the board has to act together to make the important decisions. A majority is needed to make any decision on a board, regardless of what the group is specifically discussing.

The first part of forming a board is selecting the members that will be a part of it. This is typically done by the person who founded the corporation in the first place. This individual is typically referred to as the incorporator and maybe the CEO or president of the company in question. Later on, once a board has been formed, new members can be elected onto it, not by the incorporator but by shareholders that elect and appoint them. When a board is first being formed, though, the responsibility of choosing the right members for it falls squarely on the incorporator's shoulders. The "right" members are those that the incorporator chooses for their ability to improve the company in some way and guide it in the direction they believe it needs to go. Hence, board members cannot be elected based solely on factors such as favors, friendship, or politics. Choosing a board member solely because they're your friend is a sure way to ultimately sabotage your corporation.

At the end of the day, any board member that an incorporator chooses must be capable of fulfilling the duties that they will be tasked with. To name a few examples, these duties include (*S Corp Board of Directors*, 2024):

- Establishing and writing the business' vision and mission statements and setting policies for officers and employees to follow that will enable them to achieve that vision and mission.
- Deciding on the corporation's overall policies.
- Tending to the business's legal and financial needs, such as securing loans.
- Approving the issuing of stock, deciding the salaries of executive officers, and approving shareholders' dividends.

On the whole, a board of directors' overall duty is to act in the best interest of the corporation. A typical board has four types of members. There are the ordinary board members, the chairperson of the board, the vice-chair, the board secretary, and the board treasurer. Of these, it's the chairperson of the board that leads the board.

The vice-chair acts as their second in command. The board secretary documents the minutes of board meetings, and the board treasurer oversees matters related to financial management. The precise duties of these various board members, however, are generally determined and expressed in an S-Corp's bylaws.

As you know, boards meet regularly to run their corporation. While each board meeting goes a little differently depending on what's being discussed, they do follow a traditional format. This format requires that meetings begin with a quick review of the minutes from the previous board meeting (Lander, n.d.). This is followed by a review of the report that the treasurer provides the board with. The committee reports are presented to the board, again based on what issues or matters are being discussed. That done, the process moves onto the voting stage on any old business matters that still need to be handled. Only once old business matters are tended to can the board move on to voting for new business matters. When voting is finally finished, the board usually adjourns the meeting. The secretary gathers up the minutes of said meeting as they leave so that they will be reviewed at the next board meeting.

Almost all board meetings follow this format, with the one notable exception being the first-ever meeting of a board. This is primarily because that first meeting doesn't begin with a review of the minutes, for the very simple reason that it can't by virtue of its position as the "first." After that, however, that meeting will be formatted much the same way as the ones that will come in due time. All these meetings will need to be scheduled in advance to ensure that board members are able to be there. This will also help to ensure that the necessary quora is met in these board meetings, as this is a requirement that is imposed on all S-Corps. A sound way to schedule board meetings is to send out memos and emails using something like Google Calendar. That way, you'll have physical or, rather, virtual proof that you've arranged the meeting, and you'll be able to take advantage of Google Calendar's ability to remind people of scheduled events. Thus, you'll be able to ensure that no one misses or forgets any meetings.

For the record, S-Corps don't just have to hold board meetings. They also have to regularly hold shareholder meetings at least once per year. By "have to," I mean that they are legally required to do so, and that makes sense. After all, shareholders have a vested interest in the S-Corp, and it only makes sense that they want to be kept in the loop. Like in board meetings, the minutes of shareholder meetings must be kept as well. Fortunately, shareholder and board meetings can be held on the same day. That means you can get them both out of the way around the same time and rip off the bandaid, thereby sparing yourself some time.

SUMMARY BOX

Officially launching your S-Corp can be an exhilarating thing. However, it's only the beginning of your entrepreneurial journey. Once you've taken this step, you have many more to take so you can run your new corporation and turn it into the success story you know it can be. Before we dive into how that can be done, though, let's quickly sum up what we have learned about starting your business:

- The general steps that you have to take to launch your very own S-Corporation are:
    - Choosing the perfect name for your business.
    - Filing your Articles of Incorporation.
    - Issuing your S-Corp stock.

  - Forming your board of directors and appointing your directors.
  - Making sure to meet all other S-Corp requirements.
  - Getting your Employer Identification Number (EIN).
  - Choosing your S-Corp status.
  - Getting your state and federal S-Corp licenses.
  - Creating your S-Corp bylaws.

- Articles of Incorporation typically provide the following information:

  - Your business name.
  - A short description of what your business will be doing.
  - Who your registered agent is, and what their physical address in the state is.
  - A short description of what kind of structure your business will have.

- A registered agent is an individual or business that acts as your S-Corp's formal point of contact in all legal matters.
- The individual who forms an S-Corp also forms its board. This individual is known as the incorporator.
- Once a board is formed it has to hold regular, annual meetings as required by law and keep detailed minutes of these meetings.
- S-Corps also have to hold regular shareholder meetings, which they're again required to do by law.

CHAPTER 4
UP AND RUNNING: S-CORPORATIONS

Here's the cold, hard truth: If you want your S-Corp to be truly successful, then you have to make sure that it generates between $75,000 and $250,000 in profits per owner (*S-Corp Tax Benefits*, n.d.). Otherwise, one of two things is going to happen: Either you won't be able to keep up with the costs required to keep your business going and allow it to thrive, or you will earn so little profit that your efforts simply won't be worth it. This may sound harsh, but it is true, especially if you want to be able to take proper advantage of the tax benefits that S-Corps have, which is a major part of the reason why people start S-Corps in the first place.

This, however, is just one requirement you have to meet to run a successful S-Corporation. As the owner of an S-Corporation, you will have an array of responsibilities and tasks to tend to. Some of these responsibilities will be a bit more important for your business' stability and longevity than others. The top three responsibilities you'll have to take care of as the owner of an S-Corporation are to:

- create a sound business plan.
- keep thorough records of everything.
- handle matters related to employees and budgeting.

So, why are these tasks more vital to your corporation's survival and longevity than the rest? Why are they on the very top of your to-do list and how can they help make things easier for you and your business? Let's see!

CREATING A BUSINESS PLAN

Take a look at the business world today, and you'll notice two things. The first is that there seems to be an overabundance of companies in this landscape, with new ones opening up every day. The second is that most new businesses all too often fail. Specifically, 20% of all new businesses fail within their first two years, while 45% fail within their first four years. Give it a full ten years, and 65% of all new businesses fail, no matter what business structure they have adopted (Deane, 2022). There are a myriad of reasons why new businesses can fail. One of the key reasons why S-Corporations fail, though, is that their founders and owners start them without creating any kind of business plan for themselves. That means that a lot of new S-Corps ultimately fail because they go in half-cocked, without any real idea as to what to do, how to do it, and how to properly navigate the challenges of the business world. Stumbling around blind and in the dark, is it any wonder that they hit obstacles that they cannot see and fall to the ground?

This doesn't have to be the case for you or your corporation. You have the ability to turn on the lights. You have the ability to take a proper, scrutinizing look at the business landscape you're facing, anticipate the challenges you may face, and create countermeasures against them. Despite what you may think, you don't have to be a business guru or a genius to be able to do so. All you really need to do is create a thorough and solid business plan that can act as your guide through this whole process.

Poor planning is the mother of failure, no matter what it is you're trying to do. Hence, creating a business plan is a way for you to avoid this situation. A business plan is basically a formal document that outlines what your business goals are, what strategies and methods will be used to meet those goals and the timeline that will be followed to do so. Put another way, a business plan can be considered your business' game plan or roadmap. A typical business plan consists of eight key components, these being (*What Is a Business Plan and How Do You Write One?*, n.d.):

- the business' vision and mission statements
- what services the business will be offering
- what its unique value proposition is
- who its target market is
- what its competition is like
- the business' sales and marketing strategy
- the business' financial plan
- the business' structure

The first of these components, your business' vision, and mission statements, is your starting point when working on a business plan. A vision statement is an aspirational statement that contains a phrase or two, expressing the ideal future as your business envisions it in five to ten years. Meanwhile, a mission statement is an outline, again a phrase or two, that explains what your business does and what it will be doing to turn its vision of the future into a reality. These may seem like ordinary phrases or sentences, but they are actually incredibly useful tools. They're useful because they clarify your business goals for everyone, from your employees to your shareholders and your customers. They're effective because they prove inspirational while concretely showing how your business will be achieving its long-term goals. In essence, your business' vision and mission statements are its guides, leading you toward the exact future you want.

This brings us to the next part of your business plan: the services the business will be offering. After all, it is through these services or products that your business will be achieving your vision and mission. Hence, it's important that you enumerate and detail them as much as possible. To that end, in this segment, you're going to have to detail precisely what your business will be doing. You're going to have to provide a thorough overview of all the products and services it'll be offering. Furthermore, you'll have to explain how these products and services are a part of and serve your business' vision and mission.

It's important to note here that this segment of your business plan shouldn't just include the products and services you're offering currently. It should include products and services that you intend to offer in the future as well. To that end, it should feature at least a rough timeline showing when those products and services will be put on the market. I say roughly because these timelines sometimes need to be adjusted, and you have to be flexible enough to be able to do so.

As an example of this, think back to the pandemic. If you work in the publishing industry or are an avid reader, you might have noticed that during the lockdown phase of the COVID-19 pandemic, many publishers pushed back the publication dates of their upcoming books. As such, it took an additional year for some of those books to come out. Publishers recognized that they had to make this adjustment because, with virtual events being non-existent at the time, they recognized that sticking to their current timelines would have equaled very poor sales figures for them. They also recognized that selling newer editions of previously published books, which already had name recognition among readers, would be far more profitable for them.

Once you've outlined your products and services, meaning both current and future ones, you'll be able to turn your attention to your business's unique value proposition. A business's unique value proposition is the list of benefits and advantages it will have for its customer base. In other words, it's an expression of the value the business in question will add to its customers' lives. Determining what your business value proposition will be is important because it will help you figure out how to position your corporation in the marketplace.

You can identify your business's unique value proposition by asking yourself two questions:

1. What issues or problems does your business solve for prospective customers?
2. What features do your products or services possess that'll make them stand out in the marketplace?

Asking the first question is important because it helps you to immediately see how you're going to meet customers' needs. By understanding customer problems thoroughly, you heighten your ability to solve them. You, therefore, increase customers' interest in and preference for your products and services, thereby driving sales. For this to be the case, you have to be as specific and concrete as possible while you're answering this question. You need to ensure that the problem your business is trying to solve is a top priority among your customer base. You need to phrase your value proposition in a way that highlights how your business will benefit customers, meet their needs, and resolve their issues.

As for the second question, answering it is important because odds are your business won't be the only one in the marketplace trying to solve the specific problem you've identified. If you want customers to choose your brand over others, you have to identify what your business can offer them that other businesses can't. You have to then figure that into your value proposition and ensure that it clearly explains what sets you apart from others.

Of course, identifying your value proposition becomes a great deal easier when you know exactly who your customer base consists of. This is why you need to include a target market section in your proposal. Your target market section explores the customers or potential customers who will be buying the product or service that you'll be offering them. Identifying it will enable you to zero in on their needs and problems, as well as determine their preferences, interests, and goals. Having obtained this information, you'll be able to tweak and tailor your products and services specifically to what your customers are looking for. You'll be able to change your marketing strategy to speak directly to the customers you're targeting and draw them to you by using their pain points, interests, and goals in your strategy. In keeping with that, you'll be able to refine your sales strategies in a number of ways and get to maximize your sales.

To that end, you're going to need to create a buyer persona for your target market section. Buyer persons are thorough descriptions of the different categories of customers who will be interested in your business. These categories are determined based on what each of them needs. A buyer persona typically describes a single, hypothetical individual from one category, embodying the group's general needs and characteristics. Those characteristics can be summed up as:

- demographics
- geography
- psychological components
- behaviors and attitudes

Demographics refers to a buyer persona's concrete analytical information such as their gender, age, education level, industry, job status, and nationality. Meanwhile, the persona's geographic details refer to where they live. This may include where the persona works as well if that information is pertinent to your business. Psychological components, on the other hand, are details that would affect and color the persona's preferences, needs, and wants. Such information includes their beliefs, motivations, goals, interests, passions, hopes, concerns, needs, challenges, and problems. Finally, behaviors and attitudes encompass the manner in which the persona prefers to engage with the world. Hence, they include things like the kind of content, which may be videos, audio recordings like podcasts, or written content like books and articles they consume. They also include what kind of devices, like laptops and smartphones, they use to facilitate this engagement.

The target market section of your business plan is all about collecting this vast array of information and summing it up in the fictional profiles of your buyer personas that you create. These personas will come in very handy later on, especially since you'll be able to refer back to them when developing new products and services that can appeal to the customers you're targeting.

The next part of your business plan has to do with your competition. One of the things you have to do is figure out what sets you apart from other businesses in the industry, as you'll recall. This was part of your value proposition. It is, however, a matter that merits a greater look because it can significantly improve the landscape of the market that you will be entering into. It can grant you a thorough grasp of how many competitors are out there and what products and services they are offering customers. It can, therefore, help you identify needs they're not meeting or problems they're not solving, thus making it possible for you to accomplish what they are not able to. For this to be possible, the competition-marketplace section of your business plan must answer several questions, such as:

- How many businesses and freelancers are currently in the market offering products and services that are similar to what you're offering?
- What are these businesses or freelancers doing right?
- What kinds of complaints are being made about these businesses or freelancers? What needs are they not meeting? What problems are they not solving? What are they not doing right or as best as they could?
- What does your business do or offer that other businesses in your industry can't or don't? What makes you different? How does your unique value proposition make you different?

If you've answered these questions thoroughly, then you can move on to the next section of your business plan, which concerns your marketing and sales strategies. Your buyer personas will come in very handy as you're figuring out your strategies. As an example, suppose that you're trying to figure out the best marketing strategy for a customer base that's roughly 70 years old. Odds are that this demographic won't be the most technology-savvy group out there. So, a marketing strategy that uses social media heavily won't be all that effective for them. If, on the other hand, your target demographic is around 20 years of age, then a social media marketing strategy will be the way to go. Better yet, identifying which social media platforms the demographic uses the most and designing campaigns and other sales strategies for those platforms specifically will be an immensely effective plan to go with.

The strategies you decide on for the marketing and sales section of your business plan will need to be defined very clearly in your proposal. To that end, this section will have to showcase previous successful projects and campaigns to demonstrate how they can be made use of again. It will need to detail the new strategies and techniques you'll be using, too. As you define strategies, you will need to specify exactly which communication, distribution, and sales channels you'll be using. Furthermore, you'll need to explain how you will set your sales targets, as well as how you'll achieve them.

When you're confident that you've defined your planned marketing and sales strategies as clearly and in as well-defined a manner as possible, you'll be able to start working on your business's financial plan. A sound financial plan is a must for any business that wishes to achieve long-term sustainability and success. Truthfully, a business won't start earning mountains of profits on day one of its opening. Instead, the earning process will be gradual and will require careful tracking. It will need to be a process that you plan for, to invest your capital wisely, take safety measures against unexpected circumstances and losses, and successfully balance out your expenses and earnings.

When working on your financial plan, you will need to perform a careful and thorough analysis of your business's cash flow, as well as its expenses and revenue. You will need to generate estimates for the profits you expect to earn and the losses you may incur. You will essentially need to devise a well-informed, detailed plan covering all these factors for the next few years. You will additionally have to prepare an analysis of what you have to do to break even in your business' initial years.

Based on all this information, you'll have an important decision to make if you haven't already. That decision will be your chosen business structure. This section of the business plan, therefore, declares that you intend to start an S-Corporation and potentially explore the reasons behind it, particularly the tax-related ones. Assuming you've chosen an S-Corporation, you will number among the 52.4% of all small businesses that are just starting their journey after having adopted this category for themselves (*What Is a Business Plan and How Do You Write One?* n.d.). Your business plan will conclude with this decision, thus finalizing your roadmap for the next few years and serving to draw more shareholders and investors your way if you mean to go after them.

THE IMPORTANCE OF RECORDKEEPING

The next thing you have to do once you've started your S-Corp, if you want to ensure your business's long-term well-being, is to make sure to keep thorough records. To be fair, recordkeeping isn't just vital for S-Corporations. It is of the utmost importance for any business, no matter what its size and structure are. This fact becomes especially, not to mention abundantly clear come tax season. Recordkeeping can be especially important for S-Corps, though, because they are legally required to keep detailed records of their annual board of directors meetings. That's why the minutes of those meetings are kept, as you'll recall. S-Corporations are similarly required to keep a record of the financial statements that come out of those annual meetings.

There are many other critical documents that S-Corps and other businesses have to keep records of, if only so they can avoid any future headaches. A key example of such documents is one that captures any and all transactions that your corporation engages in. Such documents include anything from receipts for business expenses to checks that your business has written (Woodman, n.d.). Your S-Corp has to keep a record of every transaction that they make, either individually or in bulk. This may get a little tedious if yours is a retail business, meaning that you engage in dozens, if not hundreds, of transactions per day. However, it will be worth it in the end.

It's not enough to just gather transactions and keep receipts in a folder. Once transactions have been gathered, they will have to be posted to your business corporate ledgers regularly. You or your bookkeeping department will have to enter these transactions into your ledgers under two separate accounts. This is what's known as double-entry booking This will ensure that records are always kept up to date and accurate.

On top of this, your S-Corporation will have to generate financial statements. One of these financial statements is your corporation's income statement. An income statement is a summary of all your business accounts. It subtracts your expense account's balance from that of your revenue account. This shows how much profit your corporation is earning. Your expense and revenue accounts are considered your corporation's temporary accounts. Your S-Corp also has permanent accounts, which are reflected in your financial statements. These permanent accounts list your assets, stockholders' equity, and liabilities. Your financial statements must list the balances of each of these assets any time they're issued, which will typically be done at the end of each accounting period for your business.

As you can see from all this, good recordkeeping will help you immensely in your effort to generate financial statements, which you will inevitably have to do. They will likewise enable you to keep track of your corporation's financial state. This will, in turn, help you spot and solve any problems in a timely fashion, as well as improve your decision-making skills as they relate to your business. Good recordkeeping will also benefit you by showing you all your sources of income. These sources won't always be immediately obvious or known to you. So, by revealing them to you, your recordkeeping habits might show you sources you hadn't been aware of. This will translate into a new income avenue you can exploit, thereby allowing you to develop new products or marketing strategies to do just that.

Most importantly, however, good recordkeeping will prove invaluable to you in tax season because it will help you to accurately prepare your tax return. Your records will also prove invaluable for the IRS in that they'll be available for the IRS to peruse. Thus, they will be able to inspect your tax returns accurately and speedily (*Why Should I Keep Records*, 2019).

Admittedly, recordkeeping can be a hard habit to fall into, especially if you've never done it before. Luckily, there are an array of apps and platforms that can help you these days. Some of the best recordkeeping apps out there are (Crawford et al., 2024):

- *Quickbooks*, which is known to be very good for all bookkeeping and recordkeeping endeavors.
- *Freshbooks*, which is especially handy for one-person businesses and freelancers.
- *Zoho Books*, which comes with a myriad of accounting-related shortcuts that make things easier for business owners.

EMPLOYEES AND BUDGETING

Finding the perfect employees for your business and figuring out their salaries, along with what yours as the owner must be, is yet another thing you'll have to do after launching your S-Corp. In S-Corporations, shareholders can also be employees of the business they're a part of. As such, shareholders who provide more than minimal service to their business and receive compensation for it are subject to federal employment taxes as the law dictates. An S-Corp owner must keep this in mind when determining their employees' reasonable wages. They must also recall that they have to pay a "reasonable salary" to themselves.

What constitutes a reasonable salary in these cases, though? A good way to figure this out is to look at what similar corporations pay individuals in similar positions, fulfilling similar responsibilities. Other factors can be considered, too. Some of these factors might be:

- What level of experience an employee has.
- What kind of training do they need.
- What their responsibilities and duties in that role will be.
- What kind of compensation agreements they have.

As you're factoring these things in, one thing you may want to do is take a look at the Bureau of Labor Statistics website. This website features extremely detailed salary information for over 800 positions. You can, therefore, use their explanations and figures as a base from which to work. You can use websites such as *Glassdoor* or *PayScale* to do a similar exercise and gain an understanding of what other players in the industry pay for certain positions.

Once you've landed on a comparable salary, you can adjust it by upscaling or downscaling it based on your corporation's status, ability, and needs. For example, if your business is smaller and less profitable than others in your field, then you likely won't be able to pay salaries that are comparable to those of other corporations. Hence, you will need to downgrade the salaries you are offering, which still remain in a fair range. One unwritten rule you might keep in mind as you work on this is that S-Corps typically split their revenue 60/40: 60% of said revenue goes out as salary, while 40% of it is treated as distributions (Fishman, 2019).

On the whole, these rules should help you immensely in determining both your employees' salaries and your own. As you work on this, however, you mustn't forget about payroll taxes. S-Corps are required by law to pay payroll taxes, which amount to 15.3% of employees' earnings. They're also supposed to pay FUTA tax, which equals 6% of the first $7,000 you make, as you'll recall. Failing to account for these as you figure out salaries can put a serious dent in your budget and mess up your financial planning for the foreseeable future. Add to that payroll services fees, which can range between $20 to $80 per month; accounting and bookkeeping fees, which can be between $20 to $70 per month; tax prep fees, which can run up to $1,500 in some cases, and annual state registration fees, which can be anywhere from $20 to $800 depending on which state you're in and things can get expensive, fast (Smiles, 2019b).

These realities, then, are all factors you have to take into account as you're trying to determine salaries, budget, and financial plans. Luckily, these don't have to run you to the ground, especially since there are a variety of things you can do to reduce your overall expenses. For starters, and perhaps most obviously, you can reduce the salary you pay to the owner. Obviously, that salary shouldn't drop below what's deemed a "reasonable" amount by the IRS, but this is likely the simplest way for you to cut costs. It is not, however, the only way. Another is to have your corporation cover the owner's health insurance premiums, assuming said owner owns more than 2% of the shares. When you do this, you gain the ability to claim a deduction for this expense you're incurring, which ultimately lessens the tax burden you'll have to bear come tax season. If you want to try this method, you can adopt it in one of two ways. You can either have the corporation reimburse the owner for their premiums or have the corporation pay them directly.

One interesting, if unexpected, method of cutting expenses is to sell your home to your S-Corp and then convert it to a rental property. This will help you save on costs since you won't have to buy or rent office space. On top of that, you'll be able to include this sale in your tax return, which will, in turn, lower your corporation's tax burden. If you are unmarried, that means you will be included in an additional $250,000 in your tax returns. If you are married, it'll mean an additional $500,000 being tacked on there (*Corporate Tax Preparation*, 2022). A similar home-related way is to claim a home-office deduction if the space you exclusively and regularly use for work is also a part of your home. This isn't just a deduction that owners can make use of but employees can as well, if they work from their room, living room, or something of the sort. Yet another home-related method is to rent your home to your corporation. This entails entering into a rental agreement with your S-Corp to rent your home to them on specific days. This allows homeowners to charge their businesses from their taxable income, thereby saving them a great deal.

Not all methods involve actual property. Some involve vehicles. As a rule, you can get a significant depreciation deduction in your first year by qualifying your "heavy" vehicle, so long as you actually use it for business purposes, like traveling back and forth between work and home. You can also receive reimbursement for your travel expenses.

There's one more thing you have to figure out to run your S-Corp effectively, and that's payroll. The first thing you need to do to set up payroll for your corporation is to file a payroll registration with your state's tax or employment agency (Rosenberg, 2023). This isn't exactly a requirement, but it is something that will allow you to do things like pay into workers' compensation insurance. Hence, it's something that will allow your corporation to receive the benefits that such useful programs have to offer.

Once you've registered your payroll, you'll move onto the business of determining reasonable compensation. You've already seen how you might go about doing that. However, if you find yourself struggling, you can always consult a seasoned tax professional, as they'll be able to provide you with significant guidance. You will also be able to make this process easier for yourself by choosing the right payroll tools and setup for you (*S Corp Payroll*, 2021). To that end, there is a variety of accounting software you can adopt. There are also a number of payroll providers out there. Getting their help in payroll matters, particularly as they relate to tax remittance, withholdings, annual tax forms, and the like, might be a good idea. After all, S-Corps typically run payroll by calculating income taxes, unemployment taxes, and FICA taxes based on wages earned. That can equal a great deal of calculating, particularly if you're a large corporation with lots of employees.

SUMMARY BOX

As you can see, there are a lot of things you need to consider and plan out carefully as you go about running your business. As you can also see, figuring out taxes often constitutes a large part of the responsibilities you have as an S-Corp owner. Taxes are a complicated matter, though. So, while they have factored into some of our discussions about S-Corps so far, they merit their own individual section, which is why we'll be focusing on them exclusively in the next chapter. Before we do that, however, let's quickly sum up what we have learned:

- The top three responsibilities you'll have to take care of as the owner of an S-Corporation are to create a business plan, keep thorough records of everything, and handle budgeting and payroll.
- An effective business plan consists of the following chapters:
    - The business' vision and mission statements.
    - What services the business will be offering.
    - What it's unique value proposition is.
    - Who its target market is.
    - What its competition is like.
    - The business' sales and marketing strategy.
    - The business' financial plan.
    - The business' structure.

- Recordkeeping can be especially important for S-Corps because they are legally required to keep detailed records of their annual board of directors meetings.
- S-Corporations have to generate financial statements. One of these financial statements is the corporation's income statement, which is a summary of all its business' accounts.
- S-Corps are required by law to pay payroll taxes, which amount to 15.3% of employees' earnings. They're also supposed to pay FUTA tax, which equals 6% of the first $7,000 you make.
- When figuring out wages, S-Corps owners must take the following into account:
  - What level of experience an employee has.
  - What kind of training do they need.
  - What their responsibilities and duties in that role will be.
  - What kind of compensation agreements do they have.
- There are a number of methods S-Corps can use to cut expenses:
  - Reducing the salary you pay to the owner.
  - Having the corporation cover the owner's health insurance premiums, assuming said owner owns more than 2% of the shares.
  - Selling your home to your S-Corp, then converting it to a rental property.
  - Entering into a rental agreement with your S-Corp to rent your home to them on specific days.
  - Claiming a home-office deduction if the space you exclusively and regularly use for work is also a part

of your home.
    - Getting a significant depreciation deduction in your first year by qualifying your "heavy" vehicle, so long as you actually use it for business purposes.

- S-Corporations should file a payroll registration with your state's tax or employment agency, though this isn't a requirement.

Share the Unknown Benefits of the S-Corp Business Structure

"The future of any corporation is as good as the value system of the leaders and followers in the organization."

LARRY ELLISON

At the start of this book, we delved into the fascinating history of S-Corps, discovering how this structure emerged in the face of concerns about the government favoring big corporate interests over small business owners. You read how the entire point of S-corps was to give smaller entrepreneurs big tax advantages… and today, over half a century down the line, millions are still reaping these rewards. The S-crop is one of the nation's most popular corporate structures, with over around 7.4 million S-corps up and running, vs only 1.7 million traditional C-corps.

Despite its considerable advantages, if one thing is clear about the process of incorporation, it's that there is no "one-size-fits-all" solution for small business entrepreneurs. This is why the very first step I invited you to take, was to ask yourself a set of vital questions to determine whether the S-corp structure was right for you. If features like pass-through taxation, limited liability corporation, and flexible ownership and management align with your goals, then I hope you are finding the information in this guide as an invaluable aid through every step of incorporation and beyond.

I can imagine you're busy gathering documentation and holding meetings to make important decisions, but I hope I can take just a couple of minutes of your time to ask you to share your opinions with others.

By writing a short review of this book on Amazon, you'll let other entrepreneurs know where they can find all the information they need to set up a legal, fully compliant S-corp.

Let them know that within these pages, they will find a complete checklist that will take them from the early stages of incorporation, all the way through to tackling taxes and beyond.

Thank you for your help. Sharing information is one of the most powerful ways to help small businesses thrive.

CHAPTER 5
TACKLING TAXES

"I love tax season. Figuring out my corporate taxes is fun to do," said no small business owner ever in the history of the world. Yet, taxes are something that all business owners have to do, no matter what business structure they've chosen for themselves. It's something that S-Corporations especially have to do, given the fact that the tax benefits that come with this business structure are part of the reason why it was chosen in the first place. Taking advantage of those benefits requires understanding them, of course, and grasping how taxes are supposed to work. Unfortunately, not everyone does, which is why 2.5% of all small businesses end up having to undergo a tax audit at some point in their lives (*7 Tips to Avoid a Small Business Tax Audit*, n.d.).

So, how exactly do taxes work for S-Corporations? What tax benefits do S-Corps actually have and how can you take advantage of them? What is an audit and why does it happen? How can you avoid an audit and what are you supposed to do if you do get audited? Without further ado, let's dive into the world of taxes to discover the answers to all these questions and more.

THE TAX PROCESS

First things first: Let's quickly go over what we know about taxes and S-Corps. As you know, S-Corps don't pay federal income taxes but may have to pay taxes at the state and local levels. The income or losses that an S-Corp earns is divided up among its shareholders. Those shareholders then report this income on their own individual tax returns. This system allows S-Corporations to avoid the dreaded double taxation that some other business structures are subjected to. For clarity's sake, double taxation happens when a corporation has to pay taxes twice in a row: once when it earns its actual income and again when they are distributing dividends to shareholders (Zaryzcki, 2022).

To be able to file taxes as an S-Corp, your business will have to elect an S-Corp status while it's being formed, as you've seen. To that end, you, as the owner, will have to file Form 2553, an Election by a Small Business Corporation. Once that's done and approved, you will be able to start filing your taxes as an S-Corp. To file your federal income tax return, you will need to file Form 1120S, U.S. Income Tax Return for an S-Corporation with the IRS come tax season. However, before you can file this form, you will need to ensure you have some specific information on hand. The key information you will need will consist of:

- Basic information regarding your business, including its name, the date on which you incorporated it, and the date when you selected your S-Corp status.
- Your Employer Identification Number (EIN).
- Your business activity code, which is a number showing what business structure you've elected for tax purposes.

- Your latest profit and loss statements, hence the importance of recordkeeping.
- Your business' balance sheet, which is a statement that lists your business' assets, liabilities, capital, and income-expenditure balance for the relevant period of time.
- Information regarding any payments you've made to any independent contractors you may have worked with that year, where you paid them a minimum of $600, and the 1099 forms that those contractors have supplied you with.

Once you have all this information on hand, you'll be able to fill out Form 1120S properly. The form will consist of four parts, these being:

- Fields A to F
- The Income Section
- The Deductions Section
- The Tax and Payments Area

Fields A to F will cover the basic information about your corporation, such as your current contact information, the dates when you incorporated and chose your S-Corp status, respectively, and a list of your S-Corp's assets. The income section will cover your business' income for the past year, which is why you'll need to have your income statements at the ready. The next section will tackle deductions, meaning your business' deductible expenses for that past year. Assuming you've taken your record-keeping activities seriously, this information should be present in your income statements as well. If you've taken recordkeeping really seriously, you'll have your receipts by your side while filling out this section, too, thereby ensuring you don't miss any critical information. The final section of the form, the tax and payments area, will tackle any and all estimated taxes you've paid that year. It will calculate what taxes you owe and what you've overpaid as you became an S-Corp.

Having filled out form Form 1120S, you will have to fill out the additional six schedules that are attached to it. To be clear, you're typically only legally required to fill out the first three schedules out of that list of six, these three being:

- Schedule B, which covers "Other Information," such as your business' accounting methods and gross receipts.
- Schedule D, which is where capital gains and losses are traditionally recorded.
- Schedule K, which bundles together all the information about your S-Corp's deductions, income, and any tax credits it qualifies for and which you will need to have on hand when putting together shareholders' Schedule K-1s, as you'll see later on.

There are three other schedules you may need to fill out, these being:

- Schedule L
- Schedule M-1
- Schedule M-2

You will only need to fill out and file Schedules L and M-1 if you've filled out Schedule B a certain way. In parts a) and b) of Schedule B, you'll encounter a question, Question 11, to be specific. If you answer this question with a "yes," then you will not need to file a Schedule L. If you answer the question with a "no," you will need to file a Schedule L. For the record, a Schedule L will allow the IRS to paint a quick picture of your S-Corporation's equity, assets, and liabilities. If you find yourself filling out a Schedule L, you'll do so using your corporation's balance sheet. As for Schedule M-1, this is where you'll report any discrepancies between the profits you've recorded in your books and those you've reported in your taxes. The same will go for any such discrepancy you pick up between the losses recorded in your books and those recorded in your taxes.

Finally, there's Schedule M-2. This is the place where you'll report any changes you've observed in the earnings that your company has retained, such as any profits you've held back so that you can reinvest them in one venture or another.

As an S-Corp, you will usually have to file Form 1120s and its necessary accompanying schedules around March 15. However, you will be able to request a six-month extension by filing Form 7004, either in person or electronically, should the need arise.

FILING ANNUAL TAX RETURNS

Now, let's get a little more detailed and take a look at how you are supposed to file your annual tax returns. The first thing you need to do for this is to prepare your financial statements and prepare them well. This means preparing your balance sheet and profit and loss statements since you'll need them to fill out your forms in the first place. Once that is done, you'll be able to move on to the next step in the process, which is to issue W-2 Forms to all your employees. In case you don't know, W-2 forms declare exactly how much compensation an employee has received that year and how much of it has been withheld by the employer so that the FICA tax on it could be paid. W-2 Forms are sent to every employee, along with a cover sheet W-3. These forms are also sent to the Social Security

Administration (SSA) and local and state governments (Lasker, 2022).

W-2 forms are additionally issued to any and all shareholders who take on management roles, seeing as they will be receiving some sort of salary. For these shareholders, box 1 of their W-2 forms will include the health insurance premiums that the S-Corp pays for them, assuming such payments are being made.

Next, the S-Corp will have to file Form 1120S, which you know how to do now. As S-Corp owners file this form, they'll get to deduct their W-2 wages on the form. Shareholders' W-2 earnings will be specified on line seven of the form, whereas that of employees will be specified on line eight.

After Form 1120S has been filed, the time will come to distribute Schedule K-1s to shareholders. Schedule K-1s are different from Schedule Ks. Schedule Ks, as you'll recall, are a part of Form 1120S and summarize the total income, credits, and deductions that are being passed on to its shareholders. Schedule K-1s, on the other hand, outline what portions of the S-Corp's earnings shareholders are responsible for paying their personal returns on, depending on what percentage of shares they possess.

As for how exactly Schedule K-1s are filled out and issued, we'll take a closer look at that momentarily. For now, let's move on to the next step, which is to file Form 1040. As you're filling out Form 1040, you'll have to enter your W-2 income in line one of the form. You'll also have to declare what portion of your S-Corp's earnings were on part two of the Dorm 1040 Schedule E. That done, you'll have to fill out Form 1040 Schedule 1, where you sum up all your supplementary income and make any final adjustments as necessary.

As you can tell from all that, this process can get a little complicated, especially if you're not well-versed in tax law. That being the case, it's typically considered a good idea for S-Corp owners to either work with a tax professional at this stage or, at the very least, use a trusted tax software that can help them navigate the process smoothly.

The good news here, though, is this: Once you've filed form 1040, you'll officially be done with taxes, at least until the next tax season rolls around. However, there is part of this process that we have glossed over and that needs to be understood better: Schedule K-1s. Hence, this part of the process requires a little more scrutiny on our part.

ISSUING K-1S TO SHAREHOLDERS

Schedule K-1s, otherwise known as 1120S K-1s since the IRS really enjoys numbering things, in case you didn't notice, are forms that record each owner's and shareholder's shares of a business' income, credits, and deductions, as previously mentioned. Hence, each shareholder and owner receives their own personal K-1 so that they can fill it out and use it to complete their tax returns. A typical K-1 is made up of three parts, these being (Rosenberg, 2022):

- Part I which asks for information about the corporation where the individual in question is a shareholder.
- Part II, which asks for information about the shareholder specifically.
- Part III, which has the shareholder declare their income for the year, their deductions, credits, and other pertinent information.

If you're an owner or an investor of an S-Corp, you will receive a K-1 as tax season nears, and you will have to file it. More importantly, you'll have to use the information that is recorded on your K-1 in your taxpayer returns, as the IRS will be on the lookout for this. It doesn't matter if you're a highly passive investor or shareholder in an S-Corp or if that corporation hasn't had a very busy year. You will still need to file your K-1 and include it in your taxpayer returns in either case.

Fortunately, K-1s aren't overly complicated forms to fill out. A K-1 consists of a single page and asks you to put your share of the income your corporation has earned. Each box on it either corresponds with one that's on Form 1040, which we've covered earlier, or to information that can be found in one of its schedules. A K-1 Form can cover a myriad of information, including royalties, qualified dividends, ordinary dividends, interest, and net short-term capital gains or losses. You can use straightforward tax software to fill out all this information. Alternatively, you can work with a good accountant. Once it has properly been filled out, you'll have to file it by around April 15 since that's typically when personal taxes are due.

STATE AND LOCAL TAXES

All of this may have covered federal taxes pretty thoroughly, but what about state and local taxes? How are S-Corps supposed to handle them? The way you tackle state and local taxes for S-Corporations varies depending on which state you're in. Typically, states adopt one of four approaches where state taxes are concerned (Corrie, 2014):

- They don't impose any entity-level taxes on S-Corporations.
- They recognize S-Corporation elections based on shareholder elections.
- They don't recognize S-Corporation elections and, therefore, tax them the way they'd tax ordinary corporations.
- They recognize S-Corps on a modified or limited basis.

What all this means is simple: Not all states immediately recognize S-Corp selections. For those that do, there is no uniform S-Corp election approval process to follow. This is why some states like New York and New Jersey require that a separate election process take place so that a corporation's status as an S-Corp can be further solidified. Other states, such as Georgia, require that shareholders who aren't Georgia residents give their permission for the corporation in question to be approved as an S-Corp. Meanwhile, some states don't recognize S-Corporation elections at all. Texas, New Hampshire, and Columbia are just a few examples of such states. They're, therefore, examples of states that do not permit S-Corps to avoid double taxation and that choose to treat them as C-Corporations instead. On top of that, certain states, such as Louisiana, tax S-Corps like they are C-Corps but allow a portion of the income that shareholders use to pay their income taxes to be excluded.

On top of all this, there are certain states that impose certain excise taxes on S-Corps. In Alabama, for example, S-Corps have to pay a business privilege tax off of their taxable net worth. S-Corps in California have to pay a 1.5% corporate franchise tax on their income. S-Corps in Ohio have to pay a 0.26% tax on their annual gross receipts. This is known as a commercial activity tax.

In all honesty, this list can go on and on, which is why any individual looking to start an S-Corporation in a specific state must look up that state's tax laws as they apply to their corporation. Otherwise, they will find themselves in unexpectedly tight corners when tax season arrives.

TAX BENEFITS: WHAT ARE DEDUCTIONS?

You might have noticed that there's one word that keeps coming up in our tax discussions: deductions. What exactly are deductions, though, and why are they important? Tax deductions are different from tax credits, another word that has come up a couple of times so far. Credits are dollar-for-dollar reductions that can be made in the amount of tax you owe for that year (Orem & Parys, 2024).

Deductions, otherwise known as write-offs, only work when they are itemized. You see, there are hundreds of different kinds of deductions an individual or corporation can claim, assuming they fit the criteria for them. The trick is to figure out which deductions your S-Corporation qualifies for and to start deducting them from your owed tax. As a rule, the more you deduct, the less you'll pay the IRS in taxes.

HOW TO TAKE ADVANTAGE OF DEDUCTIONS

That's simple enough so far, but it begs the question: How do you know which deductions your S-Corporation qualifies for? How do you then make those deductions? Oh, let me count the ways! Now, you've already seen some of the deductions that you could claim when we were discussing budgeting and cost-cutting in the previous chapter. As a reminder, one of these deductions was to reimburse your vehicle expenses, assuming you are using your personal vehicle for business purposes (*S Corp: The Best Way to Reduce Your Tax Bill*, 2023). So, what exactly can you deduct as a vehicle expense? For starters, you can absolutely deduct gas prices, especially if you drive frequently to and from, as well as to other business-related locations like fairs. You can similarly deduct your vehicle's maintenance costs and repair costs, seeing as your car will have to be in good shape for you to be able to keep using it for your work.

As always, your ability to deduct these expenses hinges on your recordkeeping. Keep the receipts of all gas runs, vehicle repairs, and maintenance trips, and you'll be able to deduct them as expenses. Keep thorough records of every time you use your vehicle for business purposes, and you'll be able to avoid any IRS scrutiny, too. The same logic applies to your travel expenses. You see, you can reimburse your travel expenses and thus increase your tax savings by turning them into deductions. Travel expenses include all manner of items such as airfare, transportation expenses, lodging, and even meals. You can deduct all these as business expenses, thereby reducing your taxable income and thus paying less tax. As with your vehicle, though, it's of the utmost importance that you keep a thorough record of all your travel expenses if you want to avoid IRS scrutiny.

Cell phone expenses can also be deducted. More specifically, a portion of the actual cost of your cell phone and the service fees can be deducted if you use it a lot for work. For this to be possible, you have to keep very accurate documents of your cell phone usage and the business-related activities you use it for. You must also remember that you can only deduct a portion of these expenses, not all of them.

There are many other deductions you can consider besides these ones. You can, for example, deduct your home office expenses, as you'll recall. You can deduct vehicle, building, and general asset depreciation, too. You can even sell or rent your home to your S-Corp, as we've explored in a previous chapter. Selling your home can save you between $250,000 to $500,000 of the income you made that year (Dutton, 2018). Renting your home can save you a great deal of money as well, but you can only rent your home for up to 14 days a year. To rent your home, you'll need to draw up the necessary paperwork to make the transaction. After that, your S-Corp will be able to deduct the rental fees for it when taxes are due.

UNDERSTANDING AUDITS

These are just some of the many ways you can take advantage of tax deductions. All of these deductions hinge on one very important factor, as you may have noticed: recordkeeping. If you want to be able to claim deductions, then you need to keep thorough, detailed records of everything. Otherwise, you won't be able to claim the deduction. You'll also find yourself in some hot water if you're ever audited.

An audit is an examination of a business' tax returns and accounting books that is done to make sure that everything is balanced and well. Typically, there are two types of audits: internal ones and ones conducted by an outside player, such as an IRS auditor. Internal audits are done by businesses themselves to ensure everything is as it should be. An external audit is one that's done to check for tax discrepancies in a business. The former is a good habit to encourage, and it's one that many firms, particularly the larger ones, do once a year to check and see if their books are accurate or not. An external audit usually takes place when the IRS realizes that there's some sort of discrepancy in your tax returns. Hence, it's a significantly more stressful proposition than the former.

As you can gather from that, most people would prefer to avoid an external audit where possible, if only so that they can avoid the stress that comes with it. Fortunately for them, there's a very sound strategy they can adopt to avoid external audits: It's to perform internal self-audits on a regular basis, ideally once a year. This way, they can head off any discrepancies they might have otherwise missed. This isn't the only benefit that comes with audits, though. There are more. For example, self-audits can boost the confidence that investors have placed in your business (Grigg, 2019). It can prove something of an assurance to potential investors, too, thereby making them more likely to put their faith in you. Similarly, self-audits can make it easy for you to spot internal troubles such as employee theft, fraud, and any major operation inefficiencies. You'll be able to nip such things in the bud after noticing them in your audit, thereby making your corporation a lot more efficient and productive.

Perhaps the most important benefit of self-audits, though, is that they make tax season a lot easier and a lot less stressful to deal with. At the very least, it will save you or, rather, your accountant a lot of time, which will be much appreciated by them.

Say that you are being audited, either internally or externally. How does that process work? To start, the auditor in question comes in, intending to perform a thorough examination of your financial statements and accounting books. To that end, they will either need your physical books or access to whatever accounting software you are using. Once they have this, they will pore over a year's worth of financial data.

As a rule, the better organized your financial data is, the easier time the auditor will have and the more quickly the whole process will go. Once the audit is over, the auditor will produce an audit report. This report will feature a statement explaining who the auditor is, what the scope of the audit was, and whether the auditor deemed the corporation's records to be fully accurate or not. Consequently, they'll take one of the following four stances about your corporation once the audit is finished:

- A clean opinion, which will state that your financial statements and books accurately and fully depict the business' financial standing.
- A qualified opinion will state that there are some points the auditor disagrees with in the financial records at hand but that the audit's scope was too limited to arrive at a definitive conclusion in the end.
- An adverse opinion, which will state that the corporation's books and financial statements misrepresent the business' financial standing to some degree.
- A disclaimer of opinion, which will state that the auditor doesn't hold any opinions on the business's financial standing.

Obviously, you want the audit report written about your business's financial standing to state a clean opinion. This goes for both internal and external audits. Having said that, it should be pointed out that IRS audits don't happen too often. In fact, less than 1% of most businesses get audited by the IRS. An IRS audit can be triggered by a select few factors. Some of these triggering factors are:

- Claiming losses for multiple years in a row.
- Claiming several deductions.

- Reporting high-income levels.
- Making an error in your tax returns that the IRS notices.

If the IRS does notice an error or discrepancy in your tax returns, they will typically send you a letter describing what they have found. If you believe that there is no real discrepancy, you can respond to this letter with evidentiary documentation at hand. If this evidence proves sufficient, then an audit likely won't take place. If not, the IRS might send an examiner to your business for a field audit. This examiner will then look through your financial records and books to ensure that you're complying with all applicable tax laws and that everything is in line with your tax returns.

SUMMARY BOX

Having discovered the secrets to navigating tax season without losing your sanity, we're now ready to move on to the intricacies that come with managing an S-Corp. By this, I mean the things you absolutely must do and the ones that you must avoid doing. As always, though, before we delve into that, let's sum up what we have discovered thus far:

- S-Corps don't pay federal income taxes but may have to pay taxes at the state and local level. The income or losses that an S-Corp earns is divided up among its shareholders. Those shareholders then report this income on their own individual tax returns.
- To be able to file taxes as an S-Corp, your business will have to elect an S-Corp status while it's being formed, as you've seen. To that end, you, as the owner, will have to file From 2553, an Election by a Small Business Corporation.

- To file your federal income tax return, you will need to file Form 1120S, U.S. Income Tax Return for an S-Corporation with the IRS come tax season.
- Having filled out form Form 1120S, you will have to fill out the additional six schedules that are attached to it. To be clear, you're typically only legally required to fill out the first three schedules out of that list of six.
- The first thing you need to do for this is to prepare your financial statements and prepare them well. This means preparing your balance sheet and profit and loss statements, since you'll need them to fill out your forms in the first place.
- The next step in the process is to issue W-2 Forms to all your employees. W-2 forms are additionally issued to any and all shareholders who take on management roles, seeing as they will be receiving some sort of salary. For these shareholders, box 1 of their W-2 forms will include the health insurance premiums that the S-Corp pays for them.
- After Form 1120S has been filed, the time will come to distribute Schedule K-1s to shareholders. Schedule K-1s are forms that record each owner's and shareholder's shares of a business' income, credits, and deductions, as previously mentioned.
- A K-1 consists of a single page and asks you to put your share of the income your corporation has earned. Each box on it either corresponds with one that's on Form 1040 or to information that can be found in one of its schedules.
- Every state has their own specific tax laws concerning S-Corporations. To be on the safe side, you must examine what your state's specific tax laws are before launching your S-Corp in said state. That way, you won't be caught off guard by unexpected taxes or be surprised when you

realize that your state taxes S-Corps the way C-Corps are taxed.

- A deduction is a small benefit that you receive by deducting a specific sum or other from your taxable income. As a rule, the more you deduct, the less you'll pay the IRS in taxes.
- Among the things you can claim tax deductions for as an S-Corp are your vehicle expenses, cell phone expenses, home office expenses, general asset depreciation, renting your home to your S-Corp, and selling your home to your S-Corp.
- An audit is an examination of a business' tax returns and accounting books that is done to make sure that everything is balanced and well. An audit can be internal or external. Internal audits are done by businesses themselves to ensure everything is as it should be. An external audit is one that's done to check for tax discrepancies in a business.
- An auditor can give one of four opinions about your corporation following an audit, these being:

    - A clean opinion, which will state that your financial statements and books accurately and fully depict the business' financial standing.
    - A qualified opinion, which will state that there are some points the auditor disagrees with in the financial records at hand but that the audit's scope was too limited to arrive at a definitive conclusion in the end.
    - An adverse opinion, which will state that the corporation's books and financial statements misrepresent the business' financial standing to some degree.

  - A disclaimer of opinion, which will state that the auditor doesn't hold any opinions on the business's financial standing.

- Less than 1% of most businesses get audited by the IRS. An IRS audit can be triggered by a select few factors. Some of these triggering factors are:

  - Claiming losses for multiple years in a row.
  - Claiming several deductions.
  - Reporting high-income levels.
  - Making an error in your tax returns that the IRS notices.

CHAPTER 6
ESSENTIAL DOS AND DON'TS

"It's not because things are difficult that we dare not venture. It's because we dare not venture that they are difficult."

SENECA

S-Corp owners have a number of responsibilities to fulfill and duties that they have to carry out, as you have seen. These essential obligations are vital for your ability to launch and run your corporation. However, they're not the only things that you need to tend to. In fact, you have an array of other peripheral tasks that will demand your attention once you start your S-Corp. These tasks may not be things you are legally required to do, but they are things that will ultimately make it easier for you to run your business and keep it alive, well, and thriving. They're things that will empower your business, thereby increasing its efficiency, productivity, and more.

Such duties are ones you must execute. In other words, they are your “dos.” Just as you have tasks you must do, you also have ones you must avoid. Such things, which we’ll be referring to as your “don’ts” are tasks, behavior patterns, and activities that will detract from your focus and energy. They’re things that risk derailing your efforts, sabotaging your work, and damaging your corporation as a whole. So, what are these dos and don’ts that you must take heed of, and why exactly are they so important? Let’s see for ourselves.

THE DOS

One of the first and arguably most important things you have to do as an S-Corp owner is to make an effort to maintain corporate formalities at all times. That means you have to do four things specifically. You have to (Morrow, 2023):

1. Regularly hold shareholders’ and directors’ meetings.
2. Document any and all decisions that are made in those meetings and save them.
3. Ensure that there’s a separation between your officers-directors-shareholders and the actual corporation.
4. Keep as detailed financial records as you possibly can.

Given all that we’ve covered so far in our book, you’re already familiar with some of these dos. Others, like ensuring there’s a separation between your officers and the actual corporation, may sound foreign to you. So what does it mean? Maintaining a separation basically means that the directors and officers of a corporation have to sign documents pertaining to the business using the corporation’s name. So, if you have a director named Matt, he cannot sign corporation-related documents as Matt. He’ll have to use the corporation’s name instead. This is valid for all sorts of documentation, such as loans, checking accounts, and other documents. It's an important rule to follow because it helps maintain liability protection. After all, if Matt were to sign a loan document using his own name, he would make himself personally liable for that loan.

Another thing you must do is to file all required tax forms, returns, and schedules on time. This includes filing your Form 1120S, Schedule B, Schedule K, Schedule K-1, Employment Tax Forms, and all necessary state tax forms that are pertinent to the state your corporation is in. To ensure that you don't miss any important forms or misfile anything, it's recommended that you work with a reputable tax professional (Steingold, n.d.). Take it from someone who has experienced firsthand how hellish figuring out corporate taxes can be: Making such an investment is absolutely worth it.

Just because you do work with a tax professional or use some kind of tax platform or software to meet your needs doesn't mean you don't need to know how corporate taxes work. In fact, you should make a point of learning all you can about tax rules as they apply to your corporation. You should especially become aware of the various tax benefits and advantages that come with being an S-Corp. That way, you'll heighten your ability to take advantage of those benefits. You'll be on the lookout for areas where you can make potential deductions. In keeping with that, you'll know to save more bills and receipts than you otherwise would have, thereby making it easier for you to claim the tax deductions you want.

There's one thing you must do before you can start thinking about taxes, though, and that's to figure out what your employees' reasonable compensation will be. It's also important to figure out what your owner's reasonable compensation as the owner of the corporation will be. These can be tricky subjects to tackle. Luckily, there are a myriad of tools and methods you can use to achieve this. For instance, looking at the wages of employees holding positions in corporations similar to yours is one of them. There are a variety of websites and resources you can use to uncover such things. Once you have, you'll be able to make better-informed decisions as you determine other people's and your own wages.

Compensation isn't the only thing you'll have to figure out, though. There's also the matter of shareholder basis. Shareholder basis refers to the amount of money a taxpayer has invested in a corporation. As an S-Corp owner, one of your responsibilities is to keep track of all shareholders on a shareholder basis. You have to monitor this year after year because this basis can prevent shareholders from making use of an S-Corporation's losses once they pass through to them. You also have to monitor this basis in case shareholders ever decide to dispose of their stock for any reason. After all, knowing the adjusted basis of shareholders will permit you to properly and accurately calculate the loss or gains of a disposition. You'll additionally make things easier for shareholders themselves because of the new rules surrounding shareholder basis. You see, a new rule was passed in 2021 that requires shareholders that meet certain specific criteria to file Form 7023, otherwise known as S Corporation Shareholder and Debt Basis Limitations, thereby reporting what their stock and debt basis are (Rodriguez, 2023).

Truth be told, there are actually two types of basis that you, as the owner of your S-Corp, will have to keep track of. These are known as the initial basis and the adjusted basis. The initial basis is the total capital contribution that a shareholder has made to your corporation in exchange for some stock ownership of it. For S-Corporations, capital contributions can mean both property, which shareholders can transfer onto them, and cash. The adjusted basis, on the other hand, is the changed version of a shareholder's initial basis, depending on what kind of income the S-Corp in question has earned or what type of losses it has incurred. If an S-Corp has earned a lot, then the adjusted basis of a shareholder will typically become higher than its initial investment. If the S-Corp has lost a lot, that shareholder's adjusted basis will be lower than what they had initially invested. When explained like that, it's easy to see why S-Corp owners have to monitor the shareholder basis closely and carefully. After all, they need to provide their shareholders with accurate information so that they can provide accurate information to the IRS.

Thus far, we've devoted ample time to the relationship between S-Corp owners and shareholders. More specifically, we've devoted a lot of time to the responsibilities that owners owe shareholders to properly run their corporations. How about owners' responsibilities toward their employees, then? Barring our discussion of wages, we've yet to really tackle this subject. An S-Corp owner has a responsibility toward their employees to pay them fair and reasonable compensation for their work. The employees are the ones that make the company run, after all. If the wages that S-Corporations offer to employees are unfair, then the employees probably won't stick with these corporations for very long. Not every S-Corporation, though, can pay astronomical wages to their employees. Some will be able to offer smaller sums compared to what their competitors can offer. This will be especially true for corporations that are small and new to the market. Fortunately, such business entities can attract employees and hold onto them using another device: employee benefits.

Employee benefits, or fringe benefits as they're otherwise known, are the various benefits that an S-Corporation can offer their employees so long as they are a part of their team. S-Corporations can later report these benefits and thus have them deducted. Such benefits are referred to as non-taxable fringe benefits, as they are deducted by employers themselves and, therefore, not reported by employees.

So, what fringe benefits can S-Corporations really offer employees? Well, first up is cafeteria plans. Cafeteria plans are written plans that allow employees to choose their compensation packages. Employees who choose this fringe benefit over compensation typically receive things like (*S-Corporation Fringe Benefits*, n.d.):

- Educational assistance, which is a written plan covering the cost of educational assistance and which affords an excludable $5,250 per employee, per annum.
- Working conditions, which define the value and quality of service of the working environment that is provided to employees so that they can perform their jobs at an optimal level and includes any training and education that's given to employees so that they can do their jobs well and better.
- Transportation and commuting benefits, which include transportation benefits that are either reimbursed or paid to employees for both commuter highway vehicles and parking and public transportation systems.
- Accident and health benefits, which is a non-discriminatory kind of health insurance that employers with more than 50 employees are required by law to offer.
- 401(k) Pension plan, which is a retirement plan where the employer makes regular contributions to employees' pensions.
- Dependent care, which is a written plan covering dependent care assistance that affords an excludable $5,000 per employee per annum.
- Group term life insurance, which is a lifelong and non-

discriminatory kind of insurance that has an excludable cost of the first $50,000.
- HSA contributions.
- FSAs.
- Simple meal plans for when they're at work, which are 50% deductible for businesses if the cafeteria is located on the business premises and additionally allows for a 50% deduction on the cost of coffee and snacks for the business.

By offering employees benefits such as these, S-Corp owners can balance out situations where they're unable to pay employees as well as other corporations can, at least for the moment. They can make the corporation itself more appealing and interesting to employees overall. Thus, they can serve to draw more talent to corporations and increase employee retention rates, along with employee motivation and productivity. During tax season, the benefits that S-Corp owners offer their employees can be turned into deductions in a variety of ways, thus lowering their taxes.

An S-Corp owner doesn't just have a responsibility toward its shareholders and employees. They have one toward themselves, too. One of their main responsibilities is to protect their personal assets. S-Corporations offer limited liability protection, as you'll recall. This is one of the reasons why many people go for S-Corporations when considering which business entity to choose for their new operations. Electing S-Corp status, however, isn't enough to fully protect your personal assets. There are other measures you must take to address this. You can start by understanding how limited liability protection works.

The limited liability that S-Corporations afford owners and shareholders protects their personal assets from loss and debt. It doesn't protect the investments they've made in the corporation. Those are fair games should a loss happen or the corporation gets into debt. There are exceptions to these rules, though. For instance, if your corporation was a sole proprietorship or an unincorporated entity that incurred debt before switching to an S-Corp model, then the owner's personal assets will remain at risk until those debts are settled. The existing debt won't pose a risk for new shareholders' or partners' assets who have joined the corporation after it became an S-Corp.

Similarly, an owner's personal assets will be at risk if they've used their personal assets to get a business loan. If that loan falls into a default, their assets may well be seized to settle the matter. In addition to this, there are cases or, rather, two very specific cases in which the limited liability protection that S-Corps have might be pierced. The first of these cases can happen when owners fail to separate their personal assets from their business assets. S-Corp owners must open up separate business accounts, as you'll remember from earlier chapters. This is so they can protect their personal assets from liability. If they fail to do so, courts can rule that the owner's business has been acting as their alter ego, thereby making their personal assets fair game. Cases like this are colloquially known as piercing the corporate veil, and it's something that owners want to avoid.

A second case in which the owner's or shareholder's personal assets are put at risk happens when owners or shareholders misbehave, so to speak. Committing misdeeds or fraud can be considered valid reasons for overcoming the limited liability protection that S-Corps usually offer (Chmielewski, n.d.).

These are all things that S-Corp owners have to be aware of if they are to properly protect their personal assets. They're things that shareholders should similarly be made aware of. A final thing that S-Corp owners must do is to document all their business expenses. The importance of proper documentation has been brought up again and again throughout the course of our book, and for good reason. You've already seen how handy proper recordkeeping can be, particularly when tax season comes around. This is because those business expenses often translate to deductibles. Deductibles can be of immense benefit to you during tax season. However, they have to be provable. Otherwise, you can't claim them, and if you do claim them without evidence, you could get into a lot of trouble (Indeed Editorial Team, 2023).

A great way to keep proper track of your business expenses is to have your department manager file monthly or even weekly expense reports. Naturally, they must keep their receipts with these reports to corroborate the expense claims made in them. Another method used in conjunction with these reports might be to have your accounting team or an accounting platform keep track of your corporation's auto-pay bills, along with any other payments that you regularly make, using their spreadsheets. These measures should create a thorough record of your expenses. Once that record is created, you can start dividing the expenses listed in them into their own categories. This can bring immediate order to your records, making them infinitely easier to navigate. Some examples of categories you might use are:

- meals
- payroll
- advertisement expenses
- travel expenses
- transportation costs

- employee benefits
- mailing and postage
- repair and maintenance expenses

Creating an organized recordkeeping system is vital, but it isn't enough. You must also create a sound approval system for the expenses your managers or employees incur. Such a system is essential for your business's ability to verify that an expense is justified. The last thing you'd want to do, after all, is claim an expense that the IRS wouldn't consider to be a deductible and, thus, get into trouble for it. As for how to create such a system, you'll have to work together with either an accounting software that you like or a good, specialized business management platform that you trust. That way, you'll be able to ensure that the system you create is easy to understand and adopt for all, as well as bulletproof.

THE DON'TS

So, those are all the things that you have to do to ensure your corporation runs smoothly. What about all the things that you must avoid doing? What do they consist of? First and foremost on this list is avoiding corporate formalities, which are things you have to do, as we have already learned. Corporate formalities encompass a number of things, from holding regular board and shareholders meetings to keeping detailed and accurate records. It's understandable why a person might be tempted to skip these formalities as they sound rather tedious. However, tedious doesn't equal unnecessary. If anything, these responsibilities are of the utmost importance if you want your business to have an actual future. Failure to comply with them may result in you and your corporation facing legal liability, which can have devastating consequences for you (Brown, 2017).

Another thing that can have pretty drastic consequences for you is to mix your personal and business accounts. Again, it's easy to see why this might be tempting for some owners, especially when they're first starting out their corporate journey. However, failing to clearly separate these two accounts from one another can have some very unpleasant repercussions. One of these is it can have legal consequences, as you know. When your personal and business accounts and assets remain entangled, any risk that's posed to your business assets and accounts affects your personal ones, too. Not only that, but this entanglement makes it easy for others to pierce the corporate veil, making things infinitely more difficult for you.

The problems that this situation creates extend beyond possible legal consequences. They carry certain tax implications, too. This is because keeping your personal and business accounts together makes it a lot harder for you to figure out your corporate and personal taxes. Consider this matter in this light: Business expenses are considered to be deductible expenses. Personal expenses, however, are not. If you are keeping your personal and business accounts together, how can you tell what's a business expense and what's a personal one? How can you separate one from the other? If this is the case, then you'll likely have a rather nightmarish time trying to separate your expenses. At the very least, you'll have to do a great deal of calculating, which can take a long time. Hence, this is typically not advisable.

As you might guess from that, keeping your accounts mixed can give rise to a significant amount of financial confusion. It can equal a lack of clarity regarding your business's financial situation and standing. This can make it very difficult for you to make good financial decisions for your business. It can lead you to make the wrong calls, which can, in turn, translate to poor business decisions and loss for all shareholders and owners involved (Hewitt, 2023).

This situation can similarly make it hard for you to manage your personal finances. Things can get so bad that you might end up in significant financial jeopardy. Your mixed accounts, for example, can mask your true financial state and cause you to overspend by giving you a false sense of reassurance. This can result in you burning through your personal funds more quickly than you otherwise would have and not realizing what you've done until it's too late.

Aside from this, your mixed accounts can spell immense trouble for you and your corporation if you're ever audited. The same goes for any instance when you're issued a regulatory compliance check. This is because both an auditor and any other regulatory examiner will expect you to keep your regulatory system clear and easy to understand, as well as thorough. If they find that to not be the case, they can fine you, launch more comprehensive investigations, and potentially take more dramatic action based on what they find.

Not keeping your accounts separate can also impede your business's financial growth. This is because potential investors will want to take a look at your financial records. Seeing your business' accounts entangled with your personal ones will hardly prove reassuring to them. If anything, it'll make them less likely to invest in your business, both because the business's financial picture will be muddied by the situation and because your choice will make you seem much less professional than you are.

One of the worst things you can do as the owner of an S-Corp is to lose your good standing with the state by failing to meet compliance requirements. There are many compliance requirements you have to meet as an S-Corp owner, like filing your annual reports. These requirements may seem small and unimportant at the time, but they can severely impact your business (CT Corporation Staff, 2018). Say that you didn't file your annual reports for a year, and no one noticed. So, you concluded it wasn't that big a deal. Then, the next year, someone picked up on what you did. In such a case, you might suddenly find yourself being slapped with a hefty fine. What's worse, you will be labeled as an increased risk by the state where your corporation operates. Hence, you might lose your Good Standing Certificate. This can become a major red flag for many. It can, therefore, cost you a great deal of business.

That's not all. Failing to meet compliance requirements may actually lead to the closure of your corporation. You'll be able to have it opened, of course, but that will take time and money. You'll have to pick a new name for your corporation and restart the incorporation process all over again. Even if that doesn't happen because you've lost your good standing with the state, you might end up losing your ability to expand your corporation into other states. This means you'll have to register your business in other states to expand its operations there. When you do, those other states will ask for your Certificate of Good Standing. You won't be able to provide them with that since you will have lost it. Those states will, therefore, not give you leave to do business within their borders.

Failing to meet compliance requirements can have a whole host of additional consequences besides this. It can prevent you from making use of the court system, which can be very problematic if you're ever sued since it'll deny you the ability to defend yourself. It can increase your personal liability, thus putting your personal assets at risk. It can cause the state to issue tax liens to you, which can prove to be very damaging. It can even lead to the dissolution of your business.

Disregarding employment taxes can have some similar consequences. This is because the IRS is allowed to pursue civil sanctions against corporations in the event that they fail to meet their employee tax obligations. They can similarly pursue criminal sanctions against owners in such cases, which can lead to their imprisonment (Salzman et al., 2018). Of course, for this to be the case, employment taxes must have been willfully avoided. That doesn't mean that unintentionally avoiding them won't have any consequences. It just means that those consequences will be a little less severe than they otherwise could have been.

What this means is pretty straightforward: If you want to avoid sanctions, you must not ignore employment taxes. Likewise, you must not ignore any changes that happen in tax law as it relates to you and your corporation. If you do, you'll typically earn a severe penalty that will be hurtful to your bottom line. This is because an ignorance of current tax law, intentional or otherwise, can result in inaccurate tax returns. If the IRS picks up on discrepancies resulting from this ignorance, which they will, they will issue a penalty to you that will equal 20% of the underpayment of the tax that took place (*Accuracy-Related Penalty*, n.d.). If you fail to pay this penalty, then it will start accruing interest. The only way to stop that from happening will be to actually pay the penalty and whatever interest it has gathered in the meantime. The penalty can be reduced if you are able to demonstrate that you were acting in good faith and genuinely unaware of any rule changes. It will not, however, be canceled even in that case.

SUMMARY BOX

There are a number of actions you must take and avoid if you want to ensure your corporation's well-being and longevity, as you have seen. Just because a corporation has a long lifespan, though, doesn't mean that they're immortal. All good things come to an end, after all, and so will any corporation once you decide to close it down. So what if you've decided that it's time to close your business down? How are you supposed to handle and navigate the closure of your S-Corp without making any mistakes? The answer to that question will be the subject matter of our next and last chapter. Before then, though, let's review what we have learned so far:

- An S-Corp owner is to make an effort to maintain corporate formalities at all times. That means you have to:
    - Regularly hold shareholders' and directors' meetings.
    - Document any and all decisions that are made in those meetings and save them.
    - Ensure that there's a separation between your officers-directors-shareholders and the actual corporation.
    - Keep as detailed financial records as you possibly can.

- Another thing you must do is to file all required tax forms, returns, and schedules on time. This includes filing your Form 1120S, Schedule B, Schedule K, Schedule K-1, Employment Tax Forms, and all necessary state tax forms that are pertinent to the state your corporation is in.
- Shareholder basis refers to the amount of money a taxpayer has invested in a corporation. As an S-Corp owner, one of your responsibilities is to keep track of all shareholders on a shareholder basis.
- Employee benefits or fringe benefits, as they're otherwise known, are the various benefits that an S-Corporation can

offer their employees so long as they are a part of their team. These benefits are deductible and serve to draw more talent and improve employee retention rates in your company.

- You must make sure to keep your personal and business accounts and assets separate at all times. Failing to do so can have some very unpleasant repercussions.
- One of the worst things you can do as the owner of an S-Corp is to lose your good standing with the state by failing to meet compliance requirements. This can cause a number of problems and result in you being issued a penalty fee, losing your Good Standing Certificate, or your corporation being dissolved.
- Disregarding employment taxes can have some similar consequences. This is because the IRS is allowed to pursue civil sanctions against corporations in the event that they fail to meet their employee tax obligations.

CHAPTER 7
DISSOLVING YOUR S-CORPORATION WITH GRACE

Here's an interesting fact: 70% of all new businesses fail within their first ten years (*Small Business Statistics 2022 Recap*, 2023). This is a troubling statistic however you look at it, as it speaks to an unfortunate truth: The odds of your first business failing for whatever reason are high. This is true for even those businesses that are built on the most promising of ideas, as I saw for myself with my first business. That's not to say that you should expect your first business to fail. It's just to say that you should be prepared for the possibility of such an eventuality coming to pass, especially considering how volatile the business world can actually be. As an extension of that, you should know how to handle your S-Corp's closure and dissolution process. That way, you can navigate that process smoothly and with minimal loss. Knowing how business closures work doesn't mean having a defeatist attitude. It simply means being prepared for the worst so that you can do your best to ensure your business is a true and resounding success.

UNDERSTANDING SMALL BUSINESS CLOSURE

An owner who is faced with the prospect of closing their business will undeniably have one overwhelming thought: I've failed. This, however, isn't necessarily the case. There can be a myriad of reasons why an owner would have to close down their business and many of these reasons stem from situations that are outside of their control. Take economic conditions, for example. Businesses can find themselves in some very unpleasant situations in times of depression or economic downturn (Vitez, n.d.).

This is especially true for businesses in specific industries like luxury goods and durable goods. In times of economic hardship, such businesses are bound to lose a large chunk of their customer base. Should this persist for long enough, they might be liable to face closure through no fault of their own. What happened to small businesses during the COVID-19 lockdowns is a prime example of that. After all, 43% of all small businesses temporarily closed down during this time, and many never reopened (Bartik et al., 2020).

Another reason why small businesses may face closure is low revenues. Businesses have a lot of expenses. Among these expenses are inventory costs, production overhead, and operating costs, to name a few. These expenses can rack up very quickly and easily. They can come to surpass the company's revenue in a surprisingly short amount of time, too. Such losses will prevent business owners from making a sufficient amount of personal income. They may also find it challenging to keep up with their business expenses. Hence, they may choose to close down their business rather than end up mired in negative profits.

Business owners might similarly close down their businesses because they simply lack the resources they need to produce and distribute their goods and services properly (Vitez, n.d.). Those resources can be anything from a talented team to natural resources needed to produce their goods and to capital to fund their endeavors. Businesses that are unable to acquire enough of these resources will ultimately have to close down their doors.

A final reason why a closure might take place has to do with fierce competition. Certain marketplaces tend to be very crowded and dominated by major players. Entering into such markets as a small, new business can be extremely tough. Think about it this way: Which small, new business do you know of that can step onto the scene and immediately start stealing away Amazon's customers? The answer to that question, in case you're wondering, is none. Businesses that are unable to compete with large companies in overcrowded industries and niches will inevitably face closure sooner or later. This is why it's important to find a niche that doesn't have lots of competition. Another reason is that finding a niche where your products/services can outperform those of the competitors can make competing against the big players as a small business possible. That being said, high competition can mean high demand. So, looking only for low-competition niches can mean lost opportunities. Especially if that niche is one that one is deeply passionate about. It would be better to find a niche you're truly passionate about and where you can make a true difference by offering something your competitors aren't, be they big or small.

A business owner might choose to close down their business for any of these aforementioned reasons. However, closures such as these won't necessarily mean that they've failed. In fact, closing down such a business can have its own unique advantages. It can, for example, allow you to sell your business and start something brand new with the money that you make. The experience you had with your business can teach you some very valuable lessons, too. These can prove to be lessons that you put to very good use in your next business venture, whatever it might be.

For this to be the case, though, you have to know when it's time to close down your business. The idea here is to choose closure yourself and not be forced into it, and the trick to do that is to recognize the signs telling you it's time to close the doors. On the whole, there are three key signs for you to take heed of, these being (*Deciding the Best Time*, 2023):

- debt
- lack of profits
- disinterest

Debt is a scary word to hear. It can cause business owners all sorts of cash flow problems and prevent them from covering their expenses as well as paying their employees' salaries. Debt can be a serious business killer in the long run, as well as an insidious one. This is because it can accumulate little by little over time. As such, a lot of owners don't realize how much of a debt problem they have until it becomes too hard to handle. That doesn't mean you should close down your business the moment you get into any kind of debt. It does, however, mean that you should keep a close eye on your debt and recognize the point when it's becoming too big of a problem for you to handle.

Another major reason for closing down a business is the lack of profits. If you're not able to generate the kind of revenue you need, are experiencing loss on a near-constant basis, or are facing a lot of debt, then those are good indicators that it's time to start thinking about closure. Why would you keep a business open, after all, if you're not actually making anything off of it?

A final sign that you're ready for closure is on the more personal side: disinterest. If you're losing or have lost your interest and passion in your work and business, then your next move should be closure. Running a business is as much an endeavor of passion as it is anything else. Your passion and interest in what you do are key motivators to keep doing it, after all. So why would you keep going if you've lost your passion and interest?

DISSOLUTION STEPS

Suppose that you've decided that it's time to close your business. How do you go about doing that and dissolving your corporation? Your first step in this regard is to get a board of directors resolution to dissolve your corporation. A board resolution is a formal document explaining the course of action a board will be taking for a business. Since dissolution is a course of action for a board to take, it's something they have to write a board resolution about. This resolution will be prepared following a formal meeting of the board where dissolution is discussed (Akalp, 2021). At this meeting, shareholders will have to vote. You will need a two-thirds majority of the votes in order to close your business. The secretary of the meeting will keep the meeting minutes as always and will, therefore, capture the results of the vote in those minutes.

Assuming you obtain the votes that you need, your next step will be to file your Articles of Dissolution with your state secretary's office. You should always double-check that you've filled out these forms correctly because any mistake made there can result in a delay in the dissolution process. On the forms, you'll indicate the date at which the dissolution of your corporation will go into effect, as determined in your board and shareholder meeting. This determined date will be some point in the future. Usually, it'll be a date that's within the first 180 days after the day you've filed your Articles of Dissolution.

Once those articles have been filed, you'll move on to notifying all your creditors, vendors, and customers about the dissolution. Some states require that you do this before filing your articles. So, you should check whether or not this is the case for your particular state. Some states additionally require that you post about your dissolution in the local newspaper. Again, you should see if yours is one of these states.

Having notified all these parties, you can now cancel all your business permits and licenses. You won't have to cancel your business' legal name with the state, seeing as filing your Articles of Dissolution should take care of that. That done, your next order of business will be to file your final payroll taxes. While you're doing that, you'll have to send W-2s and Wage and Tax Statements to all your employees for the calendar year during which they received their final wages and salaries. If you have been working with any independent contractors, you'll have to issue a Form 1099-NEC, Non-Employee Compensation, to them, assuming you've paid more than $600 to them in that past year.

Speaking of tax-related matters, you'll need to file a Form 966, which is a Corporate Dissolution or Liquidation form, with the IRS (McKeegan, 2024). This form will notify the IRS that your business is closing while giving rise to some potential tax benefits or savings for you. Having turned your attention to tax matters, you'll need to submit your final state and local sales tax forms, assuming your corporation has been collecting any sales tax on the products that it has been selling. As you're doing your federal tax returns, you'll need to select the "final tax return" box on your tax return (Akalp, 2021).

If you're all done with taxes, you'll be able to move on to selling your company's assets and liquidating them. This is especially important to do if you have any debts or creditor claims at hand. To determine the precise value of your assets, particularly any property you may have, you should speak to an intellectual property attorney. They can help you both with the sales process and with the actual transfer of the assets, which can get complicated if you are unfamiliar with it.

Once the sales and transfer process is complete, you can pay any outstanding debt you may have. If you do not have the necessary amount for this, you may want to talk to your creditors, vendors, or anyone else that debt may be owed to in order to see if they'd settle for a smaller amount. Again, you should absolutely make a lawyer part of the process you follow to settle claims. Otherwise, things can get quite complicated, really fast.

When all debts are settled and all other financial matters are out of the way, you'll be able to divide any remaining money, property, and assets among owners and shareholders. This process will usually necessitate taking into account what percentage of shares each individual owns. Ideally, your corporate bylaws will have covered how to handle this distribution process. If so, it will go a whole lot more smoothly and quickly than it otherwise would have.

The last thing you need to do to navigate the dissolution process successfully is to keep records of everything every step of the way. You should hold onto any and all employment records, financials, business tax documents, and more for years after the actual dissolution. These will be exceedingly helpful if any legal investigation is ever launched by the IRS in the future or if you just need to refer back to some key piece of information for your future endeavors.

SUMMARY BOX

Having arrived at the end of the dissolution process, you now know all that you need to do to navigate it successfully. You also know all you need to do to launch and manage your successful S-Corporation to the very end. Before we start celebrating, though, let's quickly recap what we have learned:

- Businesses can find themselves in some very unpleasant situations in times of depression or economic downturn and may face closure as a result. This is especially true for businesses in specific industries like luxury goods and durable goods.
- Another reason why small businesses may face closure has to do with low profits. Businesses have a lot of expenses. Among these expenses are inventory costs, production overheads, and operating costs, to name a few. These expenses can rack up very quickly, coming to surpass their income in the end and leading to closure.
- Certain marketplaces tend to be very crowded and dominated by major players. Entering into such markets as a small, new business can be extremely tough and may lead to the dissolution of small businesses.
- Debt can be a key reason for closure by causing business owners all sorts of cash flow problems and preventing them from covering their expenses, as well as from paying their employees' salaries.

- Another major reason for closing down a business is the lack of profits. If you're not able to generate the kind of revenue you need or are experiencing loss on a near-constant basis, then closure is a good idea.
- If you're losing interest and passion in your work and business, then your next move should be closure.
- Your first step in this regard is to get a board of directors resolution to dissolve your corporation. This resolution will be prepared following a formal meeting of the board where dissolution is discussed. At this meeting, shareholders will have to vote. You will need a two-thirds majority of the votes in order to close your business.
- Your next step will be to file your Articles of Dissolution with your state secretary's office. You should always double-check that you've filled out these forms correctly because any mistake made there can result in a delay in the dissolution process.
- You'll move on to notifying all your creditors, vendors, and customers about the dissolution. Some states require that you do this before filing your articles.
- You can now cancel all your business permits and licenses. You won't have to cancel your business' legal name with the state, seeing as filing your Articles of Dissolution should take care of that.
- Your next order of business will be to file your final payroll taxes. While you're doing that, you'll have to send W-2s and Wage and Tax Statements to all your employees for the calendar year during which they received their final wages and salaries.
- You'll need to file a Form 966, which is a Corporate Dissolution or Liquidation form, with the IRS. This form will notify the IRS that your business is closing while

giving rise to some potential tax benefits or savings for you.

- You'll next be able to move on to selling your company's assets and liquidating them. This is especially important to do if you have any debts or creditor claims at hand.
- Once the sales and transfer process is complete, you can pay any outstanding debt you may have. When all debts are settled and all other financial matters are out of the way, you'll be able to divide any remaining money, property, and assets among owners and shareholders.
- You should hold onto any and all employment records, financials, businesses tax documents, and more for years after the actual dissolution.

Help Others Achieve Their Goals

S-corps have a host of tax advantages, but they also have specific requirements that need to be strictly fulfilled. I hope this book has been an invaluable source of information as you made your way through requirements such as issuing stock certificates, filing IRS forms, and complying with ongoing requirements. If so, kindly share the things you most liked about it so that others can brave the ask of incorporation confidently and effectively.

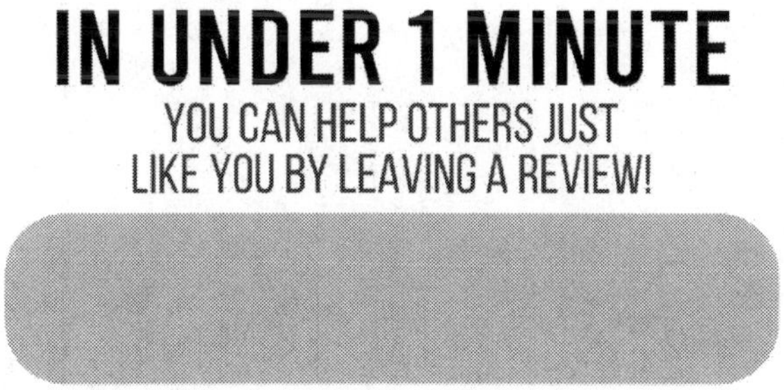

Thank you for your help. Let's show small business owners why S-corps truly provide an ideal balance between enhanced liability protection and optimal tax advantages.

CONCLUSION

Here we are, at last, at the end of the road. You've encountered and discovered a torrent of new information throughout the course of this book. You have discovered, for example, what a S-Corp truly is and what kinds of benefits it has to offer mere mortals such as ourselves. You've uncovered what makes it different from other business structures out there and what its unique advantages and disadvantages are. You've, therefore, learned how to determine whether an S-Corp truly is the right way to go for you.

Assuming you've decided that it is, in *the S-Corporations Beginners' Guide*, you've learned exactly what you need to do to launch your own S-Corp. You've seen the exact steps you need to take to start and incorporate your business, as well as the legal requirements you need to abide by to do so. You've unveiled the steps you need to take to successfully run your S-Corp without any hitches or complications. As you did so, you learned all sorts of neat skills, too, such as how to create your own business plan and master recordkeeping. As if all that weren't enough, you unearthed the secrets for tackling the leviathan known as tax season without having a heart attack over it. In the process, you even find many gems, such as tax benefits or deductions, that can help make your entrepreneurial journey significantly easier.

When you were done with that, you polished over all that information by absorbing all the things you must do and must avoid as you launch and run your S-Corporation. Thus, you put on your proverbial armor, so to speak, and made sure that you were in a prime position to weather any corporate storm. You further strengthened yourself in this regard by exploring why corporate dissolutions happen and, more importantly, how they can be navigated so that they do not damage you too badly. In doing so, you acquired the knowledge you need to fight to make your business a true unicorn while preparing for any unexpected situations that might arise along the way.

Now, here you are at the end of your journey, all geared up, having donned your armor and holding everything you need to launch your perfectly successful S-Corporation and get to work. All you need to do is turn this final page and continue along your transformative journey. Hence, there's only one last question you need to ask yourself: Are you ready to tackle this exciting new chapter of your life to come and conquer the entrepreneurial world and the industry of your choosing?

REFERENCES

Accuracy-related penalty. (n.d.). Internal Revenue Service. https://www.irs.gov/payments/accuracy-related-penalty

The advantages & disadvantages of S corporations. (2021, March 11). Smith Schafer & Associates. https://www.smithschafer.com/blog/advantages-disadvantages-of-s-corporations/

Akalp, N. (2021, October 6). *12 steps for closing a corporation by year end.* CorpNet. https://www.corpnet.com/blog/steps-closing-corporation-by-year-end/

Bartik, A. W., Bertrand, M., Cullen, Z., Glaeser, E. L., Luca, M., & Stanton, C. (2020). The impact of COVID-19 on small business outcomes and expectations. *Proceedings of the National Academy of Sciences, 117*(30). PNAS. https://doi.org/10.1073/pnas.2006991117

Benjamin Franklin's last great quote and the Constitution. (2019). National Constitution Center. https://constitutioncenter.org/blog/benjamin-franklins-last-great-quote-and-the-constitution

BrainyQuote. *Corporation Quotes.* Accessed April 4, 2024. https://www.brainyquote.com/topics/corporation-quotes

Brown, G. (2017, May 4). *What are "corporate formalities" and why do they matter?* Brown & Charbonneau, LLP. https://bc-llp.com/corporate-formalities-matter/

Bushnell Hart, A. (n.d.). Albert Bushnell Hart quotes. LinkedIn. Retrieved March 14, 2024, from https://www.linkedin.com/pulse/25-inspirational-quotes-taxes-miguel-angel-palma/

Chmielewski, T. (n.d.). *Can debtors come after the owner of a S corporation?* Chron. https://smallbusiness.chron.com/can-debtors-come-after-owner-s-corporation-46963.html

Corporate tax preparation. (2022, December 1). Molen & Associates. https://molentax.com/ten-proven-strategies-for-saving-big-money-as-an-s-corp-owner/

Corrie, T. (2014, July 9). *State tax considerations of an S corporation.* Marcum LLP. https://www.marcumllp.com/insights/state-tax-considerations-of-an-s-corporation

Crawford, H., Murphy, R., & Lauckner, S. (2024, January 2). *Best accounting and bookkeeping apps for small business*. NerdWallet. https://www.nerdwallet.com/best/small-business/accounting-bookkeeping-apps

CT Corporation Staff. (2018, July 24). *4 reasons to stay in good standing for busi-*

ness compliance. Wolter Skluwer. https://www.wolterskluwer.com/en/expert-insights/4-reasons-to-stay-in-good-standing-for-business-compliance

CT Corporation Staff. (2023, January 24). *What is a registered agent for an LLC or corporation?* Wolter Skluwer. https://www.wolterskluwer.com/en/expert-insights/what-is-a-registered-agent

De, R., & Mehran, H. (2014, November 3). *Evolution of s-corporation banks*. Liberty Street Economics. https://libertystreeteconomics.newyorkfed.org/2014/11/evolution-of-s-corporation-banks/

Deane, M. T. (2022, December 30). *Top 6 reasons new businesses fail*. Investopedia. https://www.investopedia.com/financial-edge/1010/top-6-reasons-new-busi nesses-fail.aspx#:~:text=Data%20from%20the%20BLS%20shows

Deciding the best time to open a business or close a business. (2023, May 24). Wolter Skluwer. https://www.wolterskluwer.com/en/expert-insights/choosing-the-best-time-to-open-or-close-a-business

Ditkoff, M. (2012, November 8). *50 awesome quotes on risk taking*. HuffPost. https://www.huffpost.com/entry/50-awesome-quotes-on-risk_b_2078573

Dutton, M. C. (2018, November 12). *Proven strategies to lower S corporation taxes - dutton legal group*. Dutton Legal Group LLC. https://duttonlegalgroup.com/lowering-s-corp-taxes/

Eliot, T. S. (2016, May 5). *T. S. Eliot quote*. Caren Merrick. https://carenmerrick.com/50-of-the-best-inspirational-quotes-on-taking-risks/

Fishman, S. (2019, January 24). *What is an S corp "reasonable salary"? How to pay yourself — collective*. Collective Hub. https://www.collective.com/blog/money-management/freelancers-guide-to-paying-yourself-a-salary-from-an-s-corporation

Grigg, B. A. (2019, April 12). *What is a business audit, and what types of audits should you be ready for?* Fundera.com; Fundera. https://www.fundera.com/blog/small-business-audit

Haegele, B. (2023, July 7). *How to start an S corp in 2024*. USA Today Blueprint. https://www.usatoday.com/money/blueprint/business/business-formation/how-start-s-corp/

Hewitt, J. (2023, October 14). *The vital line: Why you shouldn't mix personal and business expenses*. LinkedIn. https://www.linkedin.com/pulse/vital-line-why-you-shouldnt-mix-personal-business-expenses-hewitt-es5dc/

Hodge, S. (2014, January 13). *The U.S. has more individually owned businesses than corporations*. Tax Foundation. https://taxfoundation.org/data/all/federal/us-has-more-individually-owned-businesses-corporations/

Huston, H. (2022a, July 20). *S corporation (S corp) advantages & disadvantages| bizfilings*. Wolter Skluwer. https://www.wolterskluwer.com/en/expert-insights/s-corporation-advantages-and-disadvantages

Huston, H. (2022b, September 13). *S corp vs C corp - differences & benefits.* Wolter Skluwer. https://www.wolterskluwer.com/en/expert-insights/s-corp-vs-c-corp-differences-benefits

Indeed Editorial Team. (2023, February 4). *How to categorize small business expenses (with 20 examples).* Indeed. https://www.indeed.com/career-advice/career-development/how-to-categorize-expenses-for-small-business

Kagan, J. (2019). *What is an S corporation (S subchapter)?* Investopedia. https://www.investopedia.com/terms/s/subchapters.asp

Lander, S. (n.d.). *How to conduct board meetings for sole shareholders of S corporations.* Small Business - Chron. Retrieved March 6, 2024, from https://smallbusiness.chron.com/conduct-board-meetings-sole-shareholders-s-corporations-78451.html

Lasker, R. (2022, May 18). *A beginner's guide to S corporation taxes.* Fool. https://www.fool.com/the-ascent/small-business/articles/s-corporation-taxes/

McKeegan, D. (2024, February 1). *The essentials of form 966: Closing A company simplified.* Cleer Tax. https://www.cleer.tax/resources/form-966/

Morrow, S. (2023, January 12). *Five easy steps to maintaining your corporate status.* Legal Zoom. https://www.legalzoom.com/articles/five-easy-steps-to-maintaining-your-corporate-status

Murray, J. (2019, June 25). *7 myths about S corporations - explained.* The Balance. https://www.thebalancemoney.com/myths-about-s-corporations-explained-397381

Nelson, N. (2023, January 27). *S corp vs. LLC - differences and benefits.* Wolter Sluwer. https://www.wolterskluwer.com/en/expert-insights/s-corp-vs-llc-differences-and-benefits

Orem, T., & Parys , S. (2024, February 16). *22 popular tax deductions and tax breaks for 2023-2024.* NerdWallet. https://www.nerdwallet.com/article/taxes/tax-deductions-tax-breaks#How%20to%20claim%20tax%20deductions

Palmer, J. (2023, September 25). *What is an S corporation? (Overview and definition).* OnBoard Board Management Software | Board Portal | Board Intelligence. https://www.onboardmeetings.com/blog/what-is-an-s-corporation/

Rodriguez, N. (2023, April 24). *Basics of shareholder basis in an S corporation.* Tax pro Center | Intuit. https://accountants.intuit.com/taxprocenter/tax-law-and-news/basics-of-shareholder-basis-in-an-s-corporation/

Rogers, M. (n.d.). *Sole proprietorship vs S corp: Which is best?* Zeni AI. Retrieved March 4, 2024, from https://www.zeni.ai/blog/sole-proprietorship-vs-s-corp

Rosenberg, E. (2022, December 28). *S corp schedule K-1 (form 1120S): A simple guide.* Bench. https://www.bench.co/blog/tax-tips/form-1120s-k1

Rosenberg, E. (2023, October 30). *How to start an S corp: What you need to know.*

Collective Hub. https://www.collective.com/blog/how-to-start-an-s-corp#Set_up_payroll

S corp board of directors. (2024, January 1). UpCounsel. https://www.upcounsel.com/s-corp-board-of-directors

S corp payroll. (2021, October 28). ADP. https://www.adp.com/resources/articles-and-insights/articles/s/s-corp-payroll.aspx

S corp: The best way to reduce your tax bill. (2023, April 7). LinkedIn. https://www.linkedin.com/pulse/corp-best-way-reduce-your-tax-bill-numbersquadaccounting/

S-Corp tax benefits. (n.d.). Harbor Compliance. Retrieved March 6, 2024, from https://www.harborcompliance.com/s-corp-tax-benefits

S-Corporation fringe benefits. (n.d.). National Society of Accountants. https://www.irs.gov/pub/irs-utl/2019ntf-19.pdf

Salzman, M. L., Hibschweile, A. M., & Tedesco, M. J. (2018, February 1). *Employment tax penalties: Let's keep it civil*. The Tax Adviser. https://www.thetaxadviser.com/issues/2018/feb/employment-tax-penalties.html

7 tips to avoid a small business tax audit. (n.d.). Rocket Lawyer. Retrieved March 9, 2024, from https://www.rocketlawyer.com/business-and-contracts/business-operations/tax-audits/legal-guide/7-tips-to-avoid-a-small-business-tax-audit

Shopify Staff. (2023, September 6). *How to start an S corp: Set up an S corp in 9 steps*. Shopify. https://www.shopify.com/blog/start-s-corp

Small business statistics 2022 recap: What is the small business failure/success rate. (2023, March 21). LinkedIn. https://www.linkedin.com/pulse/small-business-statistics-2022-recap-what-failuresuccess/

Smiles, A. (2019a, May 29). *Should you start an S corp? These 4 questions will help you decide*. Gusto. https://gusto.com/resources/articles/start-business/when-start-s-corp

Smiles, A. (2019b, July 25). *Can you afford to be an S corp?* Collective Hub. https://www.collective.com/blog/business-setup/can-you-afford-to-be-an-s-corp

Staes, J. (n.d.). *S-corp history*. The S Corporation Association. https://s-corp.org/our-history/

Steingold, D. M. (n.d.). *S corporation tax filing requirements*. Nolo. https://www.nolo.com/legal-encyclopedia/s-corporations-irs-tax-filing-requirements.html

Vitez, O. (n.d.). *Reasons for closing a business*. Chron. https://smallbusiness.chron.com/reasons-closing-business-3673.html

What is a business plan and how do you write one? (n.d.). Fidelity. Retrieved March 8, 2024, from https://www.fidelity.com/learning-center/life-events/how-to-write-a-business-plan

Why should I keep records. (2019). Internal Revenue Service. https://www.irs.gov/businesses/small-businesses-self-employed/why-should-i-keep-records

Woodman, C. (n.d.). *How to adjust the balance on a profit and loss report*. Small Business - Chron.com. Retrieved March 8, 2024, from https://smallbusiness.chron.com/adjust-balance-profit-loss-report-42053.html

Zaryzcki, N. (2022, December 14). *S corporation tax filing: Benefits, deadlines, and how-to*. Bench. https://www.bench.co/blog/tax-tips/s-corp-taxes

Made in the USA
Coppell, TX
11 November 2026

11803124R00080